McGraw·Hill

SPECTRUM
SPELLING

GRADE 6

AUTHOR

Nancy Roser
Professor, Language and Literacy Studies
Department of Curriculum and Instruction
The University of Texas at Austin

**McGraw-Hill
Children's Publishing**

Columbus, Ohio

Credits

Illustrations: Steve McInturff
Electronic Illustrations: Jennie Copeland, Tom Goodwin
Heads: John Kurtz
Handwriting: Theresa Caverly

McGraw-Hill
Children's Publishing

A Division of The **McGraw·Hill** Companies

Send all inquiries to:
McGraw-Hill Children's Publishing
8787 Orion Place
Columbus, Ohio 43240-4027

ISBN 1-56189-926-7

1 2 3 4 5 6 7 8 9 10 VHS 06 05 04 03 02

How to Study a Word

1 Look at the word.

What does it mean?
How is it spelled?
Is it spelled as you expect?
Are there any unusual spellings?

disappear

2 Say the word.

What vowel and consonant sounds
do you hear?
Are there any silent letters?

disappear

dis/ap/pear

3 Think about the word.

How is each sound spelled?
Do you see any familiar word parts?

4 Write the word.

Did you copy all the letters carefully?
Did you think about the sounds
and letters?

disappear

5 Check the spelling.

Did you spell the word correctly?
Do you need to write it again?

disappear

Contents

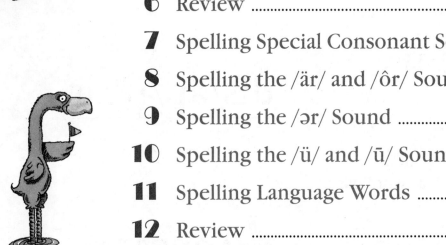

1 Spelling Short Vowel Sounds

CORE

1. unselfish
2. possible
3. accent
4. messenger
5. publish
6. snapshot
7. withstand
8. athletic
9. rapid
10. significant
11. mathematics
12. dismiss
13. penniless
14. establish
15. suspense

CHALLENGE

16. velocity
17. optimum
18. discipline
19. recommend
20. necessity

FOCUS

Sound	Sign	Spelling
short *a* and *o*	/a/ /o/	snap**shot**
short *u, e, i*	/u/ /e/ /i/	**unselfish**

Say each word. Listen for the short vowel sounds.

Study the spelling. How are the short vowel sounds *a* and *o* spelled in *snapshot*? How are the short vowel sounds *u, e,* and *i* spelled in *unselfish*?

Write the words.

1–15. Write the Core Words. Circle the letters that spell short vowel sounds.

16–20. Write the Challenge Words. Circle the letters that spell short vowel sounds.

SPELLING TIP
The short vowel sounds are often spelled *a, e, i, o,* or *u.*

WORDS and MEANINGS

Write the Core Words that best complete the story.

ONE OF BASEBALL'S FINEST

The great baseball player Satchel Paige had tremendous __(1)__ abilities. This was especially true when he stood on a pitcher's mound. During his long pitching career, Paige made a __(2)__ contribution to baseball history. Because he was able to __(3)__ the strain of pitching nearly every day, he threw in more than 2,500 games and played for 39 years. If Paige were playing today, it is __(4)__ that he would __(5)__ new records.

Although the pay in the Negro Leagues was poor, due to his fame Paige was far from __(6)__. Before each game a __(7)__ would arrive in a town and post this promise,

"Guaranteed to Strike Out the First Nine Men." The crowd would watch in __(8)__. Then, almost always, Paige would __(9)__ the batters in __(10)__ succession. Newspapers would __(11)__ breathless accounts of his amazing pitches.

No __(12)__ can show a clear picture of Satchel Paige's skills, but his __(13)__ was on pinpoint control. Those who use __(14)__ to study baseball tell us that. One batter made this generous, __(15)__ comment on Paige's pitching style, "It looked like you were winding up with a baseball and throwing a pea."

M.P.H.

The Prefix *un*- 100%

Because the prefix *un-* means "not," the Core Word *unselfish* means "not selfish." Add *un-* to each word below. Write the new word and a short definition for it.

unathletic- to not be good at athletics, un-equal- to not have the same vaulae as anoter town.

16. athletic
17. comfortable

uncofortable to not bee comfortable

18. equal
19. healthy

unhealthy not to bee in a healthy state.

20. important

unimportant not important

Run the Bases Start at home plate and follow the maze around the bases to the pitcher's mound. Find nine Core Words and write them.

1–9.

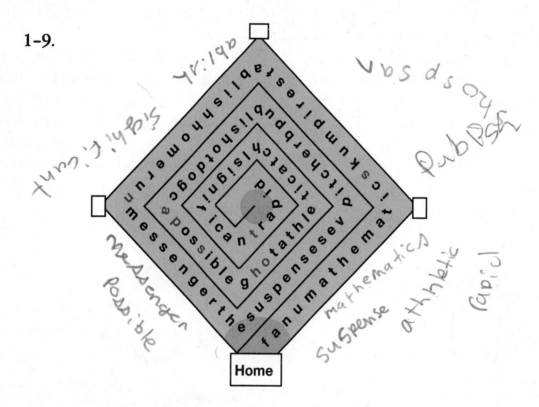

(handwritten around maze:) 86%

signature

vos dsov

publish

mathematics

athletic

rapid

suspense

messenger

possible

10. Now go around the maze again.
Build a Core Word from the red
letters and write the word. *Snapshot*

Search the Words Write a Core Word to answer each question.

11. Which word contains a smaller word that is a form of address? *dismiss*
12. Which word contains a smaller word that names a kind of fairy with magical powers? *selfish*
13. Which word begins with a smaller word that names something you write with? *penniless*
14. Which word contains a smaller word that is another name for a penny? *accent*
15. Which word contains a smaller word that is the opposite of *sit*? *withstand*

If you could interview Satchel Paige or another famous athlete for a newspaper article, what questions would you like to ask him or her? Write a list of interview questions on his or her life and career. Use at least four Core Words from this lesson.

[handwritten student notes:]
1. do you belive you could have possible a signifigan
2. how hard is it to dismis diffrence in your carrer
3. how hard is it to dismis
4. what's your fav. snapshot suspense?

Prooofreding praktices
a *c*

1–5. Here is a draft of one student's list of questions. Find five misspelled Core Words and write them correctly.

[handwritten student work on ruled paper:]

1. How did you learn to throw such rapid *rapped* pitches?

2. What was the most significant *signifecant* moment in your career?

3. Do you believe that you were born with great athletic *atheletic* skills?

4. If it were possible *posible* to sum up your life in a snapshot *snapsshot*, what would it show?

Now proofread your own list and correct any errors.

[handwritten: tommorow study words then next day test!]

CORE				CHALLENGE
unselfish	6 snapshot	11 mathematics		16 velocity
possible	7 withstand	12 dismiss		17 optimum
accent	8 athletic	13 penniless		18 discipline
messenger	9 rapid	14 establish		19 recommend
publish	10 significant	15 suspense		20 necessity

2 Spelling the Long *a, e, i,* and *o* Sounds

FOCUS

CORE

1. reply
2. snowflake
3. breathe
4. equator
5. reminder
6. theme
7. vacate ~~Cntes~~
8. devote
9. maintain
10. realize
11. rodeo
12. traitor
13. receive
14. migrate
15. release

CHALLENGE

16. microphone
17. wheelbarrow
18. supervisor
19. peculiar
20. receipt

Sound	Sign	Spelling		
long *a*	/ā/	vacate	maintain	
long *e*	/ē/	theme	breathe	receive
long *i*	/ī/	migrate	reply	
long *o*	/ō/	devote	snowflake	

Say each word. Listen for the long *a, e, i,* and *o* sounds.

Study the spelling. How are the long *a, e, i,* and *o* sounds spelled?

Write the words.

1–15. Write the Core Words. Circle the letters that spell the long *a, e, i,* or *o* sounds.

16–20. Write the Challenge Words. Circle the letters that spell the long *a, e, i,* or *o* sounds. Underline the word that has a different long vowel sound.

SPELLING TIP

The long *a, e, i,* and *o* sounds can be spelled in several ways.

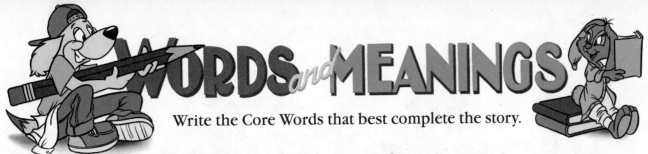

WORDS and MEANINGS

Write the Core Words that best complete the story.

WESTERN TRAVEL

Are you looking for a (1) from your daily grind? Do you wish you could (2) your regular life for a while? Well, you don't need to head for some tropical resort near the (3). Instead, travel west and experience some of our country's greatest treasures.

In the West you can (4) in the pine-scented air of the Rocky Mountains. You can (5) hours to watching what seem to be millions of stars in the big sky. You might even catch a (6) on your tongue in summer! You can watch buffalo (7) slowly across the plains.

But the West has even more to offer. If you attend a (8), you'll see riders try to (9) their seats atop bucking broncos. Or you might want to follow the trail of Jesse James, a famous (10) to the law. To quickly (11) what true adventure is, just raft down the Colorado River. Or visit the Grand Canyon, where you can shout all you want and wait for your echoes to (12). On a side trip to Arizona's Painted Desert, you could get some colored sand to take home as a (13) of your trip. The West has plenty of amusement and (14) parks to visit, too.

Everywhere you go out West, you will (15) a warm welcome. And before you know it, you'll be saying "How-dee-do!" right back.

The Noun Suffix *-ion*

When you add *-ion* to a verb, you create a noun. Change these verbs into nouns and write the nouns. Be sure to drop the final *e* before you add *-ion*.

16. devote   devotion
17. vacate   vacation
18. migrate   migration
19. create   creation
20. donate   donation

Visit the Big Sky

Study the four star groups. Then write the two Core Words that fit in each group.

1–8.

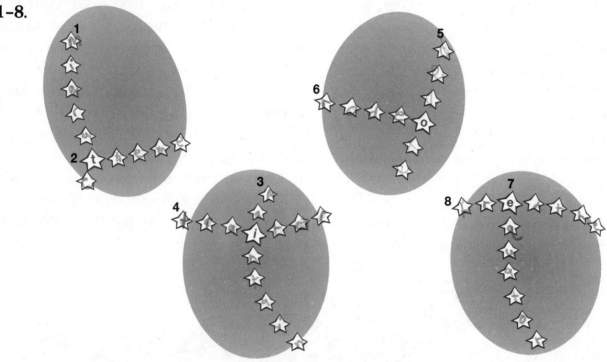

Recall the Words

Write a Core Word that begins with **re-** and matches each clue.

9. This **re-** understands completely. realize
10. This **re-** is good at letting go. release
11. This **re-** likes to get things. receive
12. This **re-** always has an answer. reply
13. This **re-** won't let you forget. reminder

Find the Hiding Places

Write a Core Word to answer each question.

14. Which word is hiding the small words *now* and *lake*? snowflake
15. Which word is hiding the word *cat*? vacate

Imagine that you are taking part in a western cattle drive. Write a letter home telling about your experience. Follow the writing process steps on pages 134–135 when you write your letter. Use at least four Core Words from this lesson.

Proofreding practicee

1–5. Here is a draft of a letter that one student wrote. Find five misspelled Core Words and write them correctly.

> Dear Mom and Dad,
>
> By the time you recieve this, I will have crossed two states. Each day I breathe a pound of trail dust. Every night I realize how tired I am. My sore legs are a reminder of the many hours I devote to sitting in the saddle. I now maintain that I would rather watch a rodeo than be a cowpoke.

Now proofread your own letter and correct any errors.

CORE			CHALLENGE
reply	6 theme	11 rodeo	16 microphone
snowflake	7 vacate	12 traitor	17 wheelbarrow
breathe	8 devote	13 receive	18 supervisor
equator	9 maintain	14 migrate	19 peculiar
reminder	10 realize	15 release	20 receipt

3 Spelling the /ô/ Sound

CORE

1. faulty
2. awning
3. haughty
4. waltz
5. launch
6. yawned
7. almanac
8. fraud
9. applaud
10. vault
11. awkward
12. haunch
13. author
14. daughter
15. laundry

CHALLENGE

16. somersault
17. laundromat
18. sauna
19. auditorium
20. inaugurate

FOCUS

Sound	Spelling
/ô/	waltz yawned
	fraud daughter

Say each word. Listen for the /ô/ sound.

Study the spelling. How is the /ô/ sound spelled in *waltz, yawned, fraud,* and *daughter*?

Write the words.

1–2. Write the Core Words that have the /ô/ sound spelled *a*.

3–5. Write the Core Words that have the /ô/ sound spelled *aw*.

6–15. Write the Core Words that have the /ô/ sound spelled *au* or *augh*.

16–20. Write the Challenge Words. Circle the letters that spell the /ô/ sound.

SPELLING TIP
The /ô/ sound can be spelled
a, aw, au, or *augh.*

WORDS and MEANINGS

Write the Core Words that best complete the story.

AN AWKWARD PARTY

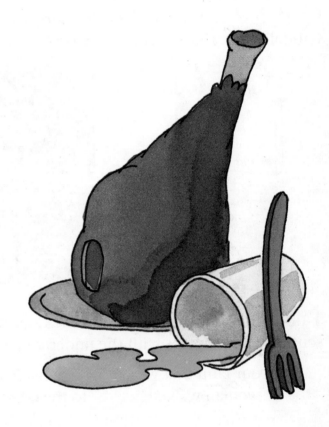

Last night Joni Dill, cookbook (1) and (2) of a famous chef, held a dinner dance. The purpose was to (3) her newest book, *Perfect Meals.* The main course was a roasted (4) of lamb. However, an (5) guest knocked the table over and sent the dishes tumbling. While the tablecloth was sent to the (6) for cleaning, guests ate lamb off their laps.

After dinner the band played a (7). Onlookers had begun to (8) the band when (9) electrical wiring caused a fire to break out. The flames spread to an (10) over the dance floor. Guests fled into a compartment, or (11), in the cellar.

One arrogant, (12) guest said it was the most dreadful event she had ever attended. She thought that Ms. Dill should be sued for (13). Another tired guest (14) and said, "This should be recorded in an (15) as the year's most disastrous dinner party."

The Endings -er and -est

Add the ending **-er** or **-est** to each base word. Write the new word. Remember to change the final *y* to *i* before adding the ending.

16. haughty + est =

17. naughty + er =

18. worthy + est =

19. dirty + er =

20. juicy + est =

Complete the Titles
Write a Core Word to complete each book title. Capitalize the first letter of the word.

1.

Dancing
the
———
by Bea
Light O'Foot

2.

What to Do
When Your
Audience
Doesn't
———
by Skip Out

3.

How to
Become an
Award
Winning
———
by I. Rhoda
Bestseller

4.

Getting
the Most
Out of an
———
by
Lotta Facks

5.

TRICKERY,
DECEPTION
& ———
by Wiley Kahn

6.

How to Get
Out of an
———
Situation
by B. Slick

Take Time to Rhyme
Write the Core Word that completes each sentence and rhymes with the underlined word.

7. It's your <u>fault</u> that we are locked inside this ———.
8. The woman walked her ——— to the edge of the <u>water</u>.

Search and Write
Write Core Words to answer the questions.

9–10. Which two words have the same spelling except for the first letter?

11–12. Which two words would be in the same word family if you added a *y* at the beginning of one of them?

13–15. Which three words end with a letter that spells the long *e* sound?

Use the Dictionary
Write the Core Words you would find on a dictionary page with the guide words shown below. Write the words in the order you would find them.

16–20. **ally/axis**

Write a diary entry describing a typical day in the life of the world's clumsiest person. Use at least four Core Words from this lesson.

Prooofreding prakticee

1–4. Here is the diary entry that one student wrote. Find four misspelled Core Words and write them correctly.

Today Anna was my partner in dance class. When we tried to waultz, I kept stepping on her toes. Later, while swing dancing, I lost my grip as I twirled Anna around. Filled with dread, I watched her launch into the dance teacher's dauter and knock her over. Anna stomped out of class, giving me a really hawty look. How akward it was!

Now proofread your own diary entry and correct any errors.

CORE			CHALLENGE
faulty	yawned	awkward	somersault
awning	almanac	haunch	laundromat
haughty	fraud	author	sauna
waltz	applaud	daughter	auditorium
launch	vault	laundry	inaugurate

4 Spelling Words with Double Consonants

FOCUS

CORE

1. hurricane
2. annual
3. vanilla
4. alligator
5. dissolve
6. pudding
7. antenna
8. commercial
9. hammock
10. innocent
11. bulletin
12. channel
13. gorilla
14. commuter
15. alley

CHALLENGE

16. parallel
17. immediate
18. corridor
19. exaggerate
20. immense

Short Vowel	Double Consonant
/a/	alley
/e/	antenna
/i/	innocent

Say each word. Listen for the vowel sound you hear before the double consonant.

Study the spelling. Notice how often double consonants follow short vowel sounds.

Write the words.

1–15. Write these headings across your paper: *dd, ll, mm, nn, rr, ss.* Under each heading write the Core Words that contain those double consonants. Circle the words that have a short vowel sound before the double consonant.

16–20. Write the Challenge Words. Circle the words that have a short vowel sound before the double consonant.

SPELLING TIP

A double consonant often follows a short vowel sound.

WORDS and MEANINGS

Write the Core Words that best complete the story.

GORILLA ON THE LOOSE!

This year, as she does every spring, Karrie visited her aunt in Florida. On the first day of her (1) vacation, Karrie lazily lay on a (2) hung between two palm trees. She was eating a bowl of (3)-flavored (4). The radio on the ground beside her was tuned to the local radio (5), WFYZ. Suddenly, an urgent news (6) interrupted a shampoo (7). "Zoo officials are warning citizens . . . " was all Karrie heard. Then the announcer's voice began to (8) in a sea of static.

Karrie adjusted the radio's long metal (9) to get better reception. The announcer went on. "The escaped animals are storming through the area faster than a tropical (10). This morning a startled (11) reported seeing a hippo racing down Highway 63. At noon an ape was spotted in an (12) behind Len's Fruit Store."

Just then Karrie heard a noise in the bushes. She glanced over and saw a scaly, green (13) creeping toward a giant, hairy (14). The look on the reptile's face was anything but (15).

Antonyms

Antonyms are words that have opposite meanings. For example, *always* and *never* are antonyms. Write an antonym for each word below.

16. innocent
17. remember
18. together
19. serious
20. imaginary

Sort the Coconuts
Sort the coconuts to form four Core Words. Use the word parts on two coconuts to form each word. You will need to use two of the coconuts twice. Write the Core Words.

1-4.

Finish the Phrase
Write a Core Word to finish each familiar phrase.

5. an ___ bystander
6. The proof is in the ___.
7. to ___ in tears
8. a notice on the ___ board
9. as strong as a 500-pound ___
10. an ___ calendar

Decode the Pictograms
Write a Core Word for each pictogram.

11.  + **enna**

12. + **etin**

13. **hurri** +

14.  + **mock**

15.  + **illa**

What do you think will happen next in the story on page 15? Write a news bulletin that gives an update of events. Follow the writing process steps on pages 134–135 to write your bulletin. Use at least four Core Words from this lesson.

Prooofreding prakticee

1–4. Here is a draft of a bulletin that one student wrote. Find four misspelled Core Words and write them correctly.

> We interrupt this comercial with a news bulletin. A girl named karrie has reported an alligator chasing a gorilla through her aunt's yard. she says the ape is now swinging from a TV antena The alligator is eating vanila pudding.

5–7. This student forgot to capitalize a proper noun and another word and left out a period. Copy the paragraph and correct the errors.

Now proofread your own bulletin and correct any errors.

CORE			CHALLENGE
hurricane	pudding	bulletin	parallel
annual	antenna	channel	immediate
vanilla	commercial	gorilla	corridor
alligator	hammock	commuter	exaggerate
dissolve	innocent	alley	immense

5 Spelling the /s/ Sound

CORE

1. specific
2. census
3. niece
4. certificate
5. circuit
6. service
7. celebrate
8. sacrifice
9. circular
10. fierce
11. cylinder
12. crevice
13. presence
14. civil
15. century

Sound	Spelling
/s/	niece civil cylinder

Say each word. Listen for the /s/ sound.

Study the spelling. How is the /s/ sound spelled in each word? What vowel follows the letter that spells the /s/ sound?

Write the words.

1–10. Write the Core Words in which the /s/ sound is spelled *c* before an *e*.

11–15. Write the Core Words in which the /s/ sound is spelled *c* before an *i* or *y*.

16–19. Write the Challenge Words in which the /s/ sound is spelled *c*. Circle the *c* that spells the /s/ sound and the vowel that follows it.

20. Write the Challenge Word that spells the /s/ sound in another way.

SPELLING TIP
The /s/ sound is sometimes spelled *c* before *e*, *i*, or *y*.

CHALLENGE

16. citation
17. cemetery
18. scent
19. ceramic
20. circumstance

Write the Core Words that best complete the story.

FIERCE GERM FIGHTERS

Every day your body's white blood cells carry out a struggle. It is as tough and (1) as any (2) war. These tiny soldiers deserve a (3) of merit because they (4) their lives to keep you healthy.

Even as you sleep, white blood cells travel along the (5) of your bloodstream. They flow into every nook and (6) of your body. Along their route the cells take a (7) of any germs they find. When they detect the (8) of many germs in one place, all of the white blood cells rush there. They then perform the invaluable (9) of fighting infection.

Imagine that you could study a sample of your blood through the long (10) of a microscope. If so, you would see that there are (11) differences between red and white cells. Red blood cells have a round, (12) shape. White blood cells, however, are shaped like blobs. This enables them to surround, attack, and destroy germs. In this way they help you to lead a longer, healthier life.

If you live for a (13), your family may gather to (14) your one-hundredth birthday. Then you can explain to each great-great-nephew and great-great-(15) that you have those tiny, loyal soldiers to thank.

The Latin Word Part *circ-*

The Latin word part *circ-* means "ring" or "circle." Write a word that begins with *circ-* to fit each meaning below.

16. a ring

17. a traveling show often performed in a round tent

18. a regular course or route

Break the Code Look at the code box. Each letter of a Core Word is represented by another letter. Use the code to write Core Words.

Code	z	y	x	w	v	u	t	s	r	q	p	o	n	m	l	k	j	i	h	g	f	e	d	c	b	a
Letter	a	b	c	d	e	f	g	h	i	j	k	l	m	n	o	p	q	r	s	t	u	v	w	x	y	z

1. xvmhfh   2. kivhvmxv   3. xbormwvi

Find the Hidden Word On a separate piece of paper, write the Core Word that fits each clue. In each word you write, circle the letter that would fall in the box. Then write the answer to question 9.

4. a very long time ⬚ _ _ _ _ _ _

5. what a beast or a wind might be _ ⬚ _ _ _ _

6. a helpful thing you might do _ _ _ ⬚ _ _ _

7. what your brother's daughter is to you _ ⬚ _ _ _

8. what you might do on your birthday _ _ ⬚ _ _ _ _ _ _

9. What is the hidden word?

Listen and Write Write Core Words to answer the question.

10–15. Which words use the letter *c* to spell the *k* sound as well as the *s* sound?

Use the Dictionary Study the pronunciation key on any page of your Speller Dictionary. Then write the Core Word for each pronunciation below.

16. /nēs/   18. /sak ′ rə fĭs/   20. /spi sif ′ ik/

17. /sil ′ ən dər/   19. /sûr ′ kit/

What if you could advertise for the things your body needs to stay healthy? Write a Help Wanted ad for one of these things. To write your ad, follow the writing process steps on pages 134-135. Use at least four Core Words from this lesson.

Proofreading practice

1-5. Here is a draft of an ad that one student wrote. Find five misspelled Core Words and write them correctly.

WANTED: White blood cells. Must have spesific germ-fighting skills. Should be fearce and have a strong sense of servise. Some sacrifise may be called for. Sircular cells need not apply. Call 555-BODY.

Now proofread your own ad and correct any errors.

CORE			CHALLENGE
specific	service	cylinder	citation
census	celebrate	crevice	cemetery
niece	sacrifice	presence	scent
certificate	circular	civil	ceramic
circuit	fierce	century	circumstance

6 REVIEW

Write a Core Word from Lesson 1 that fits each group of words. Each word you write will have a short vowel sound.

1. science, history, English, ___
2. camera, photo album, pose, ___
3. newspaper, book, print, edit, ___
4. muscular, strong, quick, ___

Write a Core Word from Lesson 2 to replace the underlined word or words below. Each word will have a long vowel sound.

5. The teacher wanted to hear the student's <u>answer</u>.
6. The <u>central idea</u> of the amusement park was space travel.
7. In the fall, some birds <u>move</u> to warm climates.
8. His note served as a <u>cause to remember</u>.

Write a Core Word from Lesson 3 for each clue below. Each word will have the /ô/ sound.

9. usually found in a bank
10. something you do after a good show
11. a trick by a cheater
12. a book of facts and other information

REVIEW

Write a Core Word from Lesson 4 to complete each sentence. Each word you write will have double consonants.

13. John was found guilty of stealing the money, but his partner was found ___.

14. It's May again, so it must be time for the ___ Garden Club Flower Show.

15. Roxanne's mother rides the ___ train to work each day.

16. Strong winds and heavy rain made this ___ one of the worst storms we've seen.

Rewrite each phrase or sentence below. Replace the underlined word or words with a Core Word from Lesson 5. Each word will have an /s/ sound spelled c. The new phrase or sentence is a famous quotation.

17. "It's safer being meek than <u>fiery and intense</u>." — ROBERT BROWNING

18. "He looked again, and found it was His sister's husband's <u>daughter of one's brother or sister</u>." — LEWIS CARROLL

19. "Every <u>one hundred years</u> has its peculiar tide of thought." — WOMAN'S RECORD

20. "Fate has always been upheld by <u>an offering without reward</u>." — SYDNEY OWENSON MORGAN

7 Spelling Special Consonant Sounds

CORE

1. thicken
2. chocolate
3. whether
4. abolish
5. chimney
6. whirlwind
7. cheddar
8. astonish
9. overwhelm
10. chamber
11. thorn
12. rubbish
13. charcoal
14. theater
15. whittle

CHALLENGE

16. shrubbery
17. chieftain
18. wharf
19. thermometer
20. mythology

24   Lesson 7

Sound	Spelling
/ch/	chamber
/sh/	rubbish
/th/	thorn
/hw/ or /w/	whittle

Say each word. Listen for the /ch/, /sh/, /th/, or /th/, and /hw/ or /w/ sounds.

Study the spellings. How is the /ch/ sound spelled in *chamber?* How is the /sh/ sound spelled in *rubbish?* How is the /th/ sound spelled in *thorn?* How is the /hw/ or /w/ sound spelled in *whether?*

Write the words.

1–5. Write the Core Words with /ch/.
6–8. Write the Core Words with /sh/.
9–12. Write the Core Words with /th/ or /th/.
13–16. Write the Core Words with /wh/ or /w/.
17–21. Write the Challenge Words. Circle the letters that spell the special consonant sounds.

SPELLING TIP

The /ch/, /sh/, /th/ or /th/, and /hw/ or /w/ sounds are often spelled *ch*, *sh*, *th*, and *wh*.

WORDS and MEANINGS

Write the Core Words that best complete the story.

TREASURE AMID THE RUBBISH

One morning Marc and I set out to search an old mining camp. Although clouds began to pile up and (1) as we hiked, the rain held off.

When we reached the camp, we found only one old cabin. Some of its walls had fallen, but the main living (2) and a fireplace with a stone (3) were still standing. We sifted through the rubble and (4) for treasure, but we found only blackened lumps of (5). Disappointed, we sat down to eat a snack of (6) cheese and (7) milk.

Suddenly, a twirling (8) of dust and debris came crashing out of the fireplace. Marc and I froze, not sure (9) to run or stay. Fear pierced my heart like a sharp (10) and threatened to (11) me. I tried to (12) my terror by squeezing my eyes shut.

Then, to my surprise, I heard Marc laugh. "Would it (13) you to know that we were terrified by a small animal?" he asked. I opened my eyes to see a very dirty raccoon in the fireplace. It faced us as boldly as if it were an actor on a (14)

stage. Then it dropped a small object and raced away.

I picked up the object. It was a beautifully carved wooden figure that must have taken someone ages to (15). I found myself wondering what the story behind it might be. But then I saw a tattered note attached to it.

Homophones

Homophones are words that sound alike but have different spellings and meanings. Write a homophone for each word below.

16. whether   18. witch   20. serial

17. steal   19. bored

Decode the Stones

Each stone on the chimney holds a word and a number. If the number in a stone is 1, write down the first letter of the word in the stone. If the number is 2, write down the second letter, and so on. Then use the letters from the row of stones to write a Core Word.

1-5.

star 2	ache 3	oboe 1	bear 4	snap 2
mean 3	stub 4	dots 2	lend 1	rise 2	case 3	hand 1
rest 4	cash 4	mild 2	face 3	park 4	when 3	next 1
adds 1	asks 2	most 4	soap 2	dine 3	idea 1	dust 3	rich 4
mice 3	hope 1	shop 3	coin 1	loop 2	pull 4	bats 2	trap 1	feed 3

Take a Close Look

Write Core Words to answer each question.

6-8. Which three words have a short vowel sound before a double consonant?

9. Which word has the long *e* sound spelled *ey*?

10-11. Which two words spell the long *o* sound in different ways?

12. Which word has the same final consonant blend as the word *blend?*

13-15. Which three words end with the /ər/ sound spelled *er?*

Use the Dictionary

Look up each Core Word below in your Speller Dictionary. Write each word and draw a line between the syllables.

o/ver/whelm

16. astonish 17. chocolate 18. thicken 19. abolish 20. theater

What do you think the note in the story on page 25 might have said? Write a note that could have been attached to the carved figure. Follow the writing process steps on pages 134–135 to write your note. Use at least four Core Words from this lesson.

Prooofreding prakticee
a (above "o"), c (above "k")

1–4. Here is a draft of one student's note. Find four misspelled Core Words and write them correctly.

> I do not know wether anyone will find this figure.
> if so, do not dismiss it as rubbich. I worked hard
> to wittle it, and it carries a secret that will
> astonich you A bag of gold lies inside the chimney
> beside my humble carving

5–7. This student forgot to capitalize one letter and left out two periods. Copy the note and correct the errors.

Now proofread your own note and correct any errors.

CORE			CHALLENGE
thicken	whirlwind	thorn	shrubbery
chocolate	cheddar	rubbish	chieftain
whether	astonish	charcoal	wharf
abolish	overwhelm	theater	thermometer
chimney	chamber	whittle	mythology

8 Spelling the /är/ and /ôr/ Sounds

CORE

1. discard
2. origin
3. barge
4. formula
5. guitar
6. ornament
7. harness
8. fortress
9. departure
10. organize
11. carbon
12. fortunate
13. partially
14. ordinary
15. pardon

CHALLENGE

16. quarantine
17. torment
18. formation
19. assortment
20. cordial

Sound	Spelling
/är/	carbon
/ôr/	fortress

Say each word. Listen for the /är/ sound you hear in *carbon*. Listen for the /ôr/ sound you hear in *fortress*.

Study the spelling. How is the /är/ sound spelled in *carbon*? How is the /ôr/ sound spelled in *fortress*?

Write the words.

  1–8. Write the Core Words that have the /är/ sound. Circle the letters that spell the /är/ sound.

 9–15. Write the Core Words that have the /ôr/ sound. Circle the letters that spell the /ôr/ sound.

16–20. Write the Challenge Words. Circle the letters that spell the /ôr/ sound. Underline the word that has the /ôr/ sound spelled *uar*.

SPELLING TIP
The /är/ sound is often spelled *ar*.
The /ôr/ sound is often spelled *or*.

WORDS and MEANINGS

Write the Core Words that best complete the story.

PLANNING THE CLASS SHOW

On Tuesday we held a meeting to decide what kind of class show to put on this year. We hoped the meeting would help us (1) our ideas so we could focus on some and (2) others.

Our past shows had been successful. The usual (3) for their success had involved a talent show. Most of us thought we should do that again. This year Juanda Perez offered to play her (4). Sam Cook said he could draw "magic pictures" using (5) paper. Others offered to sing or dance. Everybody felt (6) to have so much talent in the class! And our teacher noted that the show would be a perfect way to (7) our energy.

Then, begging our (8), Gil Mehta broke in. He said that what we were planning was very dull and (9). He suggested something quite different. Gil wanted to put on a class play. In fact, he had written one. It was set in the Middle Ages and had knights defending a (10) high on a hill while their king sailed away on a (11). Gil said that the sets were already (12) built, and that we would need only to add an (13) here and there.

Gil argued his plan well. Before we took our (14) from the meeting, we cast a vote. Gil's plan won, and that was the (15) of our class play!

The Suffix -ate

The suffix -ate can be used to form adjectives or verbs from nouns. For example, *fortunate* is an adjective formed from the noun *fortune* plus -ate. Write the word formed by adding -ate to each noun below.

16. carbon   17. origin   18. formula

Find the Missing Letters
Figure out the missing letters and write the Core Words. Then use the letters that would go inside the armor to write the answer to question 6.

1. c _ _ _ _ _

2. _ _ _ i _ _ _

3. _ _ _ d _ _

4. _ _ _ t _ _

5. _ _ g _ _ _ _

6. What might knights use to escape by sea?

Take a Close Look
Write Core Words to answer the questions.

7–8. Write the two Core Words you could change from nouns to adjectives by adding the suffix **-al.** Then write each word with the **-al** suffix added to it.

9–10. Which two words spell the /ch/ sound with *t?*

11. Which word spells the /sh/ sound with *t?*

Complete the Category
Write the Core Word that belongs in each group.

12. castle, palace, ___

13. saddle, bridle, ___

14. reject, throw away, ___

15. recipe, mixture, ___

30   **Lesson 8**

WRITE ON YOUR OWN

Write a description of your own plan for a great class show. Follow the writing process steps on pages 134–135 to write your description. Use at least four Core Words from this lesson.

Proofreding prakticee

1–4. Here is a draft of one student's description. Find four misspelled Core Words and write them correctly.

My class show will be anything but oardinary. Since we are fortunate enough to have some class clowns among us, I would oreganize a comedy show. Students would do funny skits. There would be comics and mimes, too. It would be a real diparture from the same old boring foremula!

Now proofread your own description and correct any errors.

CORE			CHALLENGE
discard	ornament	carbon	quarantine
origin	harness	fortunate	torment
barge	fortress	partially	formation
formula	departure	ordinary	assortment
guitar	organize	pardon	cordial

Spelling the /ər/ Sound

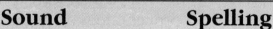

CORE

1. yogurt
2. calendar
3. desperate
4. surrender
5. accurate
6. surveying
7. capture
8. popular
9. barrier
10. familiar
11. emperor
12. alternate
13. pressure
14. admiral
15. memory

CHALLENGE

16. survivor
17. burglar
18. perpetual
19. calculator
20. monitor

Sound	Spelling		
/ər/	calendar	barrier	admiral
	memory	yogurt	pressure

Say each word. Listen for the /ər/ sound you hear in *calendar*.

Study the spelling. How is the /ər/ sound spelled in *calendar, barrier, admiral, memory, yogurt,* and *pressure*?

Write the words.

1–15. Write the Core Words. Circle the letters that spell the /ər/ sound. Underline the word that spells the /ər/ sound in two different ways.

16–20. Write the Challenge Words. Circle the letters that spell the /ər/ sound.

SPELLING TIP
The /ər/ sound can be spelled *ar, er, ir, or, ur,* or *ure.*

WORDS and MEANINGS

Write the Core Words that best complete the story.

THE EMPEROR OF YOGURT

Once upon a time, if you believe in such tales, there was an empire called Monopolis. An old and wise (1) known as Monos ruled the land. As time passed and Monos marked more years off the (2), he grew (3) to find the fountain of youth.

One day Monos sent for the (4) of his navy. Monos told the skipper to travel the world and to (5) anyone who knew the secret of eternal life. The loyal skipper replied, "No (6) shall be too high to stop me. I shall not (7) my goal until your bidding is done."

Years went by, and the (8) to beat the clock grew. Monos spent each day (9) the sea, waiting for his navy's return. His moods began to (10) between hope and despair. Monos never lost his sharp (11) and still cared for his people. As a result he remained a (12) ruler.

At long last the fleet returned, and the skipper approached Monos. "After traveling the globe," the seafarer said, "I have learned that eating (13) is the secret to eternal life." Monos waited not a minute before he began consuming great amounts of the stuff.

Now, anyone (14) with this story knows that this must indeed be an (15) formula for long life. For today, Monos still rules Monopolis.

Words from Foreign Languages

Many of our food words come from other languages. For example, the word *yogurt* is a Turkish word. Write the English word that fits each definition and origin below.

16. a breakfast food, from Dutch *wafel*

17. a long, thin pasta, from Italian *spago*

18. ground beef, from German *Hamburg*

Finish the Program Write the Core Word that best completes each song title on the talent show program. Begin each Core Word with a capital letter.

♪♪ **TALENT SHOW** | **PROGRAM** ♪♪

1. "I Can't Erase the _____ of You" by The Forget-Me-Nots
2. "Please _____ Your Heart to Me" by the Lovin' Soldiers
3. "No _____ 's Too High to Stop Our Love" by the Hurdlers

4. "Will We Ever _____ That Feeling Again?" By The Regretfuls
5. "Can I Be the _____ of Your Fleet?" By The Seafarers
6. "You're the _____ of the Empire of My Heart" by The Humble Subjects

Get to the Core Write Core Words to answer the questions.

7. Which word has a base word that means "to look at or study in detail"?
8. Which word has a base word that means "push"?
9. Which is the only word with a long *o* sound?
10. Which word is pronounced one way when it is a verb and another way when it is a noun or an adjective?
11–12. Which two words could you make into nouns by adding the suffix *-ity?*
13. Which word contains the smaller word *lend?*
14–15. Which two words contain the smaller word *rate?*

Use the Dictionary A dictionary entry sometimes includes a sentence to show the meaning of the entry word. Use each word below in a sentence that shows the word's meaning. Write the sentences.

16. familiar   17. desperate   18. accurate   19. popular   20. pressure

Write an ad for a brand of yogurt called NatureFresh. Make the product sound as appealing as possible. Follow the Steps in the Writing Process on pages 134–135 to write your ad. Use at least four Core Words from this lesson.

Prooofreding prakticee

1-4. Here is a draft of one student's ad. Find four misspelled Core Words and write them correctly.

SURRENDER YOUR TASTE BUDS TO NATUREFRESH YOGURT

Are you seeking an altirnate to fatty dairy foods? Look no further than our populer Nature-Fresh yogurt. We believe it is accureate to say that Nature-Fresh is tastier than any other yogurt. So try it! It's sure to capshur your fancy.

Now proofread your own ad and correct any errors.

CORE			CHALLENGE
yogurt	surveying	emperor	survivor
calendar	capture	alternate	burglar
desperate	popular	pressure	perpetual
surrender	barrier	admiral	calculator
accurate	familiar	memory	monitor

10 Spelling the /ü/ and /ū/ Sounds

CORE

1. unruly
2. youth
3. lagoon
4. duplicate
5. numerous
6. solitude
7. caboose
8. group
9. nuisance
10. union
11. routine
12. suitable
13. jewelry
14. improve
15. consume

CHALLENGE

16. souvenir
17. crusader
18. neutral
19. illuminate
20. shrewd

FOCUS

Sound	Spelling		
/ü/	unruly	consume	improve
	nuisance	lagoon	caboose
	group	jewelry	
/ū/	union	youth	

Say each word. Listen for the /ü/ and /ū/ sounds.

Study the spelling. How is the /ü/ or /ū/ sound spelled in each word?

Write the words.

1–13. Write the Core Words that have the /ü/ sound. Circle the letters that spell the /ü/ sound.

14–15. Write the Core Words that have the /ū/ sound. Circle the letters that spell the /ū/ sound.

16–20. Write the Challenge Words. Circle the letters that spell the /ü/ sound. Underline the word that spells the /ü/ sound *eu*.

SPELLING TIP
The /ü/ sound can be spelled
u, u-e, o-e, ui, oo, oo-e, ou, or *ew.*
The /ū/ sound can be spelled *u* or *you.*

WORDS and MEANINGS

Write the Core Words that best complete the story.

Jobs in Photography

Does a career in photography interest you? If so, there are (1) kinds of photography jobs for you to consider.

You could, for example, be a nature photographer and visit exotic places like Africa. There you might get a great shot of a (2) of zebras drinking from a blue (3). Or you could capture the moment when an (4) family of monkeys are about to (5) a lunch of grass and roots.

Would you like to photograph things such as diamond (6) for ads? If so, you may want to become a commercial photographer. Or you could be an art photographer and take pictures of subjects as varied as a vase of flowers or an old train (7).

No matter what field of photography you decide to enter, you can choose to work alone in (8) or in (9) with fellow artists. However, be sure to take courses early on, while you are still in your (10). Learn the (11) of how to take, develop, and copy or (12) your own pictures. Find out which subjects are (13) for photographing and which are nothing but a (14) to shoot. As you use roll after roll of film, your skills will steadily (15).

The Noun Suffix *-ment*

The noun suffix *-ment* can add the meaning "the product or result of " to a verb. For example, *improvement* means "the product or result of improving." Add *-ment* to each verb below.

16. ail

17. pave

18. amend

19. enjoy

20. state

Lesson 10   37

Name the Photos

Each picture below needs a one-word title. Write the Core Word that makes the best title. Capitalize the first letter of the title.

1.

2.

3.

4.

5.

Take Time to Rhyme

Write Core Words to create rhymes.

6. a runaway railroad car: a loose ___
7. what the Tooth Fairy gets from a child: a ___ tooth
8. the kind of chowder served to a crowd: ___ soup
9. what a fake ruby necklace is called: ___ foolery
10. what people aged 13 to 19 do every day: a teen ___
11. an action taken to try to do better: a move to ___

Think and Write

Write Core Words to answer the questions.

12. Which word has a prefix that means "not" or "the opposite of "?
13. Which word is a synonym of *many?*
14. Which word is a synonym of *pest* or *bother?*
15. Which word has a base word that means "be right for" and a suffix that means "likely to"?

Write a journal entry describing a day in the life of a nature photographer in Africa. Follow the writing process steps on pages 134–135 to write your entry. Use at least four Core Words from this lesson.

Prooofreding prakticee

1–5. Here is a draft of one student's journal entry. Find five misspelled Core Words and write them correctly.

> Today I got some shots of a group of hippos sitting in a lagoone. I've made friends with neumerous monkeys, but one is quite an unruley nuisance. This morning I saw it steal some of my duiplicate photos and consume all of my lettuce. I hope things will impruve.

Now proofread your own journal entry and correct any errors.

CORE			CHALLENGE
unruly	solitude	routine	souvenir
youth	caboose	suitable	crusader
lagoon	group	jewelry	neutral
duplicate	nuisance	improve	illuminate
numerous	union	consume	shrewd

11 Spelling Language Words

CORE

1. vowel
2. contraction
3. pronoun
4. adjective
5. comma
6. predicate
7. adverb
8. English
9. conjunction
10. article
11. essay
12. consonant
13. syllable
14. preposition
15. hyphen

FOCUS

Say each word. Listen for the vowel and consonant sounds. Do you hear any short or long vowels? Do you hear the /ou/ sound?

Study the spelling. Look for familiar spelling patterns. Are short vowels spelled with a single letter? Is the /ou/ sound spelled *ow* or *ou?* Are there unusual spellings?

Write the words.

1–15. Write the Core Words in alphabetical order. Circle any familiar spellings. Underline any unusual spellings.

16–20. Write the Challenge Words. Circle any familiar spellings. Underline any unusual spellings.

SPELLING TIP
Many language words have familiar spellings. Others have spellings that must be remembered.

CHALLENGE

16. participle
17. infinitive
18. phrase
19. interjection
20. punctuation

WORDS and MEANINGS

Write the Core Words that best complete the story.

Experts on the English Language

A copy editor's job is to fix errors in a piece of writing such as an (1) or an (2). Good copy editors must have a strong grasp of the (3) language.

Copy editors must know the rules of punctuation in order to spot and correct punctuation errors. For example, if the (4) between the day of the month and a year is missing, the editor adds it. When a word that has more than one (5) must be divided between two lines, the editor adds a (6). When words such as *is* and *not* are joined in a (7), the editor makes sure that the apostrophe is placed correctly. Copy editors also look for spelling errors. No letter, whether a (8) or a (9), escapes their gaze.

Copy editors use a different set of rules to correct grammar. For example, every sentence must have a subject and a (10). If a subject is compound, the simple subjects must be linked by a (11) such as *and*. But that's not all! An (12) such as *quick* must not be confused with the (13) *quickly*. A (14), such as *he* or *they*, must relate to a noun in a clear way. Also, it is difficult to read a sentence that ends with a (15), such as *of* or *with*.

As you can see, rules are a copy editor's tools. Does this type of "repair work" interest you?

Plurals

To form the plural of most nouns that end in a vowel and *y*, you simply add *s*. But if the noun ends in a consonant and *y*, you must change the *y* to *i* and add *es*. Write the plural of each noun below.

16. essay
17. colony
18. monkey
19. decoy
20. rally

Peek into a Poem
Each underlined word is a certain part of speech or type of word. Write a Core Word to name the parts of speech.

1. Our language is a very <u>strange</u> thing.
2. You <u>can't</u> say "brang" but can say "bring."
3. Why are there "geese" <u>but</u> never "gooses"?
   Why not say "meese" <u>or</u> even "mooses"?
4. Why does plain "I" turn <u>into</u> "me"?
5. Why isn't "us" the same <u>as</u> "we"?
6. Who made these rules, I'd <u>badly</u> like to ask,
7. Because learning them is quite <u>a</u> task.

Name the Clues
Write the Core Word that names each clue.

8. b, d, f, p, or z
9. a, e, i, o, or u
10. sub -ject
11. Hey who are you? ,
12. twenty - two
13. John lives in California.

Think and Write
Write the Core Word that completes each statement.

14. *Spain* is to *Spanish* as *England* is to ___.
15. *Ant* is to *insect* as ___ is to *writing*.

Use the Dictionary
Words can have more than one meaning. Look up each underlined Core Word in your Speller Dictionary. Write the definition that shows how the word is used in the sentence.

16. I just read an <u>article</u> on grizzly bears.
17. *Doesn't* is a <u>contraction</u> of *does not*.
18. They worked in <u>conjunction</u> with others.

If you could write some new rules for the English language, what would they be? Write a list of new and surprising rules for our language. Use at least four Core Words from this lesson.

Proofreding praktice

1-4. Here is a draft of the rules that one student wrote. Find four misspelled words and write them correctly.

1. The consonunt "z" will be dropped.

2. The pronoun "I" will be written "i."

3. The adjictive "cute" will no longer exist.

4. There will be no wrong way to spell or write Inglish.

Now proofread your own list of rules and correct any errors.

CORE			CHALLENGE
vowel	predicate	essay	participle
contraction	adverb	consonant	infinitive
pronoun	English	syllable	phrase
adjective	conjunction	preposition	interjection
comma	article	hyphen	punctuation

Write a Core Word from Lesson 7 for each clue below. Each word will have a /sh/, /th/, or /ch/ sound.

1. another word for garbage
2. the sharp part of a rose bush
3. smoke leaves the house through this
4. the place where a movie is shown

Rewrite each phrase or sentence below. Replace the underlined word or words with a Core Word from Lesson 8. Each word will have an /är/ or an /ôr/ sound. The corrected phrase or sentence is a famous quotation.

5. "The everyday or commonplace changes of nature, which are in themselves equally wonderful, are disregarded."
— ALMIRA LINCOLN PHELPS

6. "The first who was king was a lucky soldier." — VOLTAIRE

7 "Forgive or allow one offense, and you encourage the commission of many." — PUBLILIUS SYRUS

8. "The Owl looked up to the stars above,
And sang to a small stringed instrument." —EDWARD LEAR

Write a Core Word from Lesson 9 that means the opposite of each word below. Each word you write will have an /ər/ sound.

9. resist
10. incorrect
11. strange
12. release

Write a Core Word from Lesson 10 to complete each sentence. Each word will have a /ü/ or /ū/ sound and rhyme with the underlined word.

13. If you drank all the water from a shallow body of water, you would consume the ___ .

14. If the last car on the train were unhooked, you'd have a loose ___ .

15. A crowd eating broth is a soup ___ .

16. An enclosure for children is a ___ booth.

Write a Core Word from Lesson 11 that describes the underlined word in each sentence below. Each word you write is used to talk about the English language.

17. Joan can't attend the meeting.

18. A bird in the hand is worth two in the bush.

19. She said they were with him.

20. "...and that government of the people, by the people and for the people shall not perish from the earth."

13 Easily Misspelled Words

CORE

1. guest
2. knead
3. salmon
4. knelt
5. guardian
6. wholly
7. honesty
8. khaki
9. herb
10. solemn
11. knuckle
12. wholesome
13. hustle
14. gnash
15. whom

CHALLENGE

16. guarantee
17. rhinoceros
18. knowledge
19. spaghetti
20. rhinestone

FOCUS

Sound	Spelling
/nēd/	knead
/hüm/	whom

Say each word. Listen for familiar vowel and consonant sounds in each word.

Study the spelling. Which letters are silent in each word? Which other Core Words have the same silent letter patterns?

Write the words.

1–10. Write these headings across the top of your paper: *kn, gu, wh, kh, mn,* and *gn.* Under each heading, write the Core Words that contain those spelling patterns.

11–15. Write the other Core Words. Circle the silent letters in each word.

16–20. Write the Challenge Words. Circle any unexpected spellings you see in each word.

SPELLING TIP
Some words are easily misspelled. You must find strategies to remember their unexpected spellings.

WORDS and MEANINGS

Write the Core Words that best complete the story.

WHOLESOME, DELICIOUS BREAD

If you want to try your hand at baking bread, start with a recipe for wheat bread. Wheat bread is easy to make as well as being healthful and (1). It goes well with any main course, from beef to (2).

To begin you need to gather and mix the basic ingredients. Then add a pinch of your favorite spice or (3). Next, mix and (4) the dough with the heel of your hand, hitting the dough now and then with your palm or (5). Work it for ten minutes, until the dough is a light (6) color and (7) free of air bubbles. Let the mixture rise in a pan, then (8) it quickly into the oven before the dough falls.

In all (9), making bread can be tricky. So if your bread doesn't come out right the first time, don't fret and (10) your teeth. There are some people to (11) this skill comes easily, but others may need practice. You may hover beside your oven, serious and (12), feeling like the appointed (13) of the loaves. But remember, many others have (14) by their ovens like you, anxiously waiting and watching. And many a dinner (15) has been delighted with what those ovens produced!

Unusual Plural Forms

Some nouns have unusual plural forms. For example, the plural of *salmon* is *salmon*. Write the plural form of each noun below.

16. ox

17. scissors

18. child

19. foot

20. cactus

Lesson 13   47

Have Fun with Puns

A pun is a joke in which a word has two meanings. Write a Core Word to complete each pun. Begin your answer to question 5 with a capital letter.

1. What did the baker say to her assistant?
   "I ___ bread."
2. What did the father say about his son's tattered jeans?
   "Those pants are ___ unwearable."
3. What did one generous innkeeper say to another?
   "Your ___ is as good as mine."
4. What did the mouse say as it ate Swiss cheese?
   "This cheese is mighty ___."
5. What did the submarine captain say to his cousin Herbert?
   "I live in a sub, ___."

Think and Write

On a separate piece of paper, write a Core Word to fit each clue. The silent letter in the word is given.

6. yellowish brown _ h _ _ _
7. serious _ _ _ _ _ n
8. to grind teeth g _ _ _ _
9. protector _ u _ _ _ _ _ _
10. truthfulness h _ _ _ _ _ _
11. finger joint k _ _ _ _ _ _

Solve the Puzzle

On a separate piece of paper, write the Core Words that solve the puzzle.

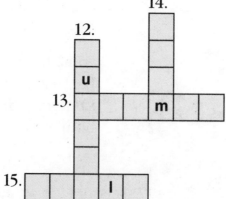

Imagine that you are in a kitchen where bread is baking. Write a paragraph that describes what you see, smell, and feel. Follow the writing process steps on pages 134–135 to write your description. Use at least four Core Words from this lesson.

Prooofreding prakticee

1–5. Here is a draft of one student's description. Find five misspelled Core Words and write them correctly.

> I hustle into the kitchen, and the holesome smell of baking bread greets me. A hint of herb is in the warm air. The room is a kaki color, and it welcomes me like a long-lost gest. A cat sits by the oven like a solem guardian. I feel holey relaxed and calm, but I am also filled with hunger.

Now proofread your own description and correct any errors.

CORE			CHALLENGE
guest	wholly	knuckle	guarantee
knead	honesty	wholesome	rhinoceros
salmon	khaki	hustle	knowledge
knelt	herb	gnash	spaghetti
guardian	solemn	whom	rhinestone

14 Spelling Words That End with -ous

CORE

1. tremendous
2. famous
3. ridiculous
4. dangerous
5. jealous
6. adventurous
7. mountainous
8. vigorous
9. courteous
10. previous
11. continuous
12. humorous
13. nervous
14. disastrous
15. vicious

CHALLENGE

16. treacherous
17. boisterous
18. venomous
19. ambitious
20. mischievous

Say each word. Listen for the final sounds.

Study the spelling. How is the ending of each word alike? Do you see a base word in any of the words?

Write the words.

1-4. Write the Core Words in which -ous was simply added to a base word.

5-9. Write the Core Words in which a final e was dropped from the base word when -ous was added.

10-15. Write the other Core Words. Circle any familiar word parts you see in these words.

16-20. Write the Challenge Words. Circle the -ous ending in each word.

SPELLING TIP
The -ous ending is simply added to some words. When -ous is added to a word ending in e, the e is dropped. Some words with -ous do not have familiar base words.

WORDS and MEANINGS

Write the Core Words that best complete the story.

Another Disastrous Vacation

My family is (1) for telling funny stories about our vacations. Each trip is a bigger disaster than the last one. But the most (2) one of all was our camping trip to Mount Rainier.

Mom, who is always energetic and (3), thanks to her job as a gym teacher, made us hike miles each day. We felt as if we were on a nonstop, (4) treadmill. My sister, who isn't exactly an expert on (5) manners, finally refused to walk another inch. I had to keep hiking, and I felt (6) that she had escaped the treks but I hadn't.

The next day, though, Mom gave up hiking when we met a bear. It seemed as (7) as a giant redwood! But luckily the bear was neither (8) nor (9). In fact <u>it</u> ran away from <u>us</u>!

Mom, still feeling daring and (10), decided we'd do some driving instead. Now, Mount Rainier is 14,410 feet high— high enough to put the "mount" in (11). Everything was fine until we started

heading down. Then the car's brakes began to fail, making us really (12). Dad, who had spent the (13) few days reading in the tent, finally leaped into action. He yanked on the emergency brake, jumped out, and stopped the car with some big rocks.

You may think this was (14) of us, but we have now given up camping forever. This story may seem (15), but the trip itself was anything but funny.

DANGEROUS CURVES AHEAD!

Changing Adjectives into Nouns

All the Core Words are adjectives. Follow the directions below to change each Core Word into a noun.

16. jealous + y

17. famous - ous + e

18. courteous - ous + sy

19. disastrous - rous + er

20. vicious + ness

Finish the Signs

Each sign below is missing one word. Write the Core Word that best completes the sign. Capitalize the first letter of each word.

1. **Terrain Ahead**

2. **Come See World-_____ Mount Rushmore!**

3. **Tours from 9 a.m. to 5 p.m.**

4. **Trail: Keep _____ Away!**

5. **Please Be _____ and DON'T LITTER**

Look and Listen

Write Core Words to answer the questions.

6. Which four-syllable word has two short *i* sounds?
7. Which three-syllable word has the /z/ sound spelled with an *s?*
8. Which four-syllable word has the /ch/ sound spelled with a *t?*
9–10. Which three-syllable words have the /ər/ sound spelled *or?*

Search for Words

Find five Core Words in this word-search puzzle. They may be spelled across or down. Write the words on a separate piece of paper.

11–15.

```
r f w o l p u d n t x
j y m n a r c o v l i
e t r e m e n d o u s
a u n e r v o u s m f
l s a b w i l x d e r
o v i c i o u s p n y
u j w k q u t c h z e
s o y b l s x q u f t
```

Write the first paragraph of a story about a mountain-climbing adventure. Make your opening a "cliff-hanger" that will leave readers in suspense. Follow the writing process steps on pages 134–135 to write your paragraph. Use at least four Core Words from this lesson.

Proofreading practice

1–4. Here is a draft of one student's story opening. Find four misspelled Core Words and write them correctly.

> Kyle knew from his preveous climbs that Eagle Mountain was dangerous. This time, though, his climb was nearly disasterous. His trouble began when he climbed the famous eastern slope. Halfway up, he heard a continueous rumbling sound. Then he saw a tremendus boulder rushing toward him.

Now proofread your own story opening and correct any errors.

CORE			CHALLENGE
tremendous	adventurous	continuous	treacherous
famous	mountainous	humorous	boisterous
ridiculous	vigorous	nervous	venomous
dangerous	courteous	disastrous	ambitious
jealous	previous	vicious	mischievous

15 Spelling the /k/ Sound

CORE

1. scheme
2. chaos
3. bouquet
4. character
5. headache
6. schedule
7. technique
8. chemistry
9. mechanic
10. orchestra
11. chlorine
12. mosquito
13. chrome
14. monarchy
15. chorus

CHALLENGE

16. chromosome
17. zucchini
18. chrysanthemum
19. scholarship
20. chronological

Sound	Spelling
/k/	chaos mosquito

Say each word. Listen for the /k/ sound you hear in *chaos* and *mosquito*.

Study the spelling. How is the /k/ sound spelled in *chaos, headache,* and *schedule?* How is the /k/ sound spelled in *mosquito* and *bouquet?*

Write the words.

1–3. Write the Core Words with /k/ spelled *qu.*

4–16. Write the Core Words with /k/ spelled *ch.*

17–21. Write the Challenge Words. Circle the letters that spell the /k/ sound.

SPELLING TIP
The /k/ sound is sometimes spelled *ch* or *qu.*

WORDS and MEANINGS

Write the Core Words that best complete the story.

A HELPFUL HEADACHE

Maria had a summer job working in her Uncle Rafael's laboratory. He was developing a method, or (1), for recycling the (2) from old car bumpers.

Thanks to a friend who was an auto (3), the lab was filled with old car parts. The jumble of bumpers, soap, (4), beakers, and (5) books gave it an air of (6). The mess just confirmed Maria's beliefs that her uncle was an odd (7) whose latest crazy (8) would never work. She kept her thoughts to herself, though, and quietly followed his hectic, round-the-clock (9).

Then one day Maria developed a splitting (10). She took a break and sat on a pile of bumpers. Closing her eyes, she imagined herself standing in front of a symphony (11). She had just sung a solo, backed up by an opera (12). Now a member of the (13)—perhaps the queen herself—was handing Maria a (14) of roses. At that moment a (15) buzzed Maria's ear.

Maria awoke from her daydream feeling full of resolve. It was time to quit her lab job. After all, she wanted to be a singer, not an inventor!

Plurals of Nouns Ending in *o*

To form the plural of a noun that ends in *o*, you add *-s* or *-es*. Write the plural of each noun below.

16. mosquito + es
17. echo + es
18. zero + s
19. hero + es

20. radio + s
21. piano + s
22. tomato + es

Mix and Match
Match a syllable from bumper 1 with a syllable from bumper 2 and a syllable from bumper 3. Write the Core Words you make.

1–4.

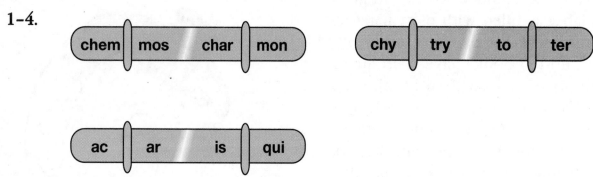

Solve the Letter Puzzles
Write the Core Word that fits each clue.

5. It has *n, c, h,* and *m,* but no *y.*
6. It has *t, h, c,* and *s,* but no *i.*
7. It has *o, s, h,* and *c,* but no *a.*
8. It has *c, i, r,* and *h,* but no *m.*
9. It has *h, a, c,* and *o,* but no *r.*

Think and Write
Write Core Words to answer the questions below.

10. Which word has only one vowel sound, the long *o* sound?
11. Which word has only one vowel sound, the long *e* sound?
12. Which word spells the /j/ sound with a *d?*
13–14. Which two two-syllable words are stressed on the second syllable?
15. Which word is a compound word that has a short *e* spelled *ea?*

Use the Dictionary
Look up each of the following words in your Speller Dictionary. Write each part of speech that the word can be.

16. chorus 17. schedule 18. scheme

What daydreams have you had about doing unlikely, unique, or impossible things? Write a list of your wildest daydreams or make some up. Use at least four Core Words from this lesson.

Prooofreding prakticee

a c

1–5. Here is a draft of one student's list. Find five misspelled Core Words and write them correctly.

My daydreams are to :
– become a member of the British monarky.
– win the Nobel Prize in kemistry.
– sing backup korus for a famous singer.
– become a mekanic on a rocket to mars.
– breed a hardy type of moschito that won't bite.

6. This student forgot to capitalize one proper noun. Copy the list and correct all errors.

Now proofread your own list and correct any errors.

CORE			CHALLENGE
scheme	schedule	chlorine	chromosome
chaos	technique	mosquito	zucchini
bouquet	chemistry	chrome	chrysanthemum
character	mechanic	monarchy	scholarship
headache	orchestra	chorus	chronological

16 Spelling Words with Negative Prefixes

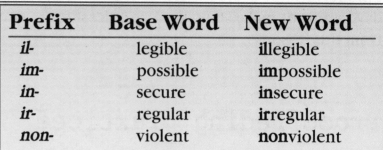

FOCUS

CORE

1. illegible
2. irrational
3. nonviolent
4. illegal
5. irregular
6. impossible
7. insecure
8. nonprofit
9. impartial
10. illiterate
11. independent
12. impatient
13. nonstandard
14. incorrect
15. illogical

CHALLENGE

16. irresponsible
17. inconclusive
18. inescapable
19. impersonal
20. incapable

Prefix	Base Word	New Word
il-	legible	illegible
im-	possible	impossible
in-	secure	insecure
ir-	regular	irregular
non-	violent	nonviolent

Say each word. Listen for the prefix in the first syllable.

Study the spelling. Does the spelling of each base word change when the prefix is added? Does the meaning change?

Write the words.

1–15. Write these headings across the top of your paper: *il-, im-, in-, ir-, non-*. Under each heading write the Core Words that contain that prefix. Circle each prefix.

16–20. Write the Challenge Words. Circle each prefix.

SPELLING TIP
The spelling of many base words does not change when the prefix *il-, im-, in-, ir-,* or *non-* is added.

WORDS and MEANINGS

Write the Core Words that best complete the story.

AN INDEPENDENT PET

Anyone getting a puppy must be prepared to spend a lot of time with it. Some dogs are secure and (1), but others need constant attention. If you are (2) to pedigrees, you may wish to get your puppy from a (3) organization such as an animal shelter. Just remember that the dog is likely to be nervous and (4) in a new home. Try not to be overeager or (5). Gaining a puppy's trust will take time.

Right away, you'll need to get a dog license. An animal control officer may consider an animal (6) if it doesn't have one. Also ask a vet what your dog's normal diet should be. If it eats (7) or (8) foods, it may get sick.

The next step is to train your pet. Dogs may be (9) when it comes to knowing the alphabet, but they *can* learn the difference between correct and (10) behavior. A good way to start training a dog is to try thinking like one. You'll soon realize that what seems logical and

rational to us may seem (11) and (12) to a puppy. For example, a sign saying "Keep off the grass" is (13) to a dog. So of course the dog will run across the lawn! Don't punish your pet for what it doesn't know. And when you *must* correct it, do so in a gentle, (14) way. If you follow this rule, it will be nearly (15) to go wrong.

The Suffixes *-ent* and *-ence*
The suffix *-ent* is an adjective suffix. The suffix *-ence* is a noun suffix. Replace the adjective suffixes below with noun suffixes. Write the nouns.

16. impatient

17. nonviolent

18. independent

19. incident

20. convenient

Switch and Write Replace the underlined word or words in each speech balloon with a Core Word with the same meaning. Write the new sentences.

1. Those judges were certainly **unbiased**.

2. Fifi, your stance is **wrong**.

3. Holding dog shows in the rain ought to be **against the law**.

4. Fido, your signature on this entry form is **not readable**.

Use the Clues Write a Core Word that has the given prefix and fits the clue.

5. This *ir-* is never sensible.
6. This *im-* just can't stand to wait.
7. This *il-* cannot reason correctly.
8. This *in-* wants to do things its own way.
9. This *non-* is always gentle.
10. This *non-* likes to be different.
11. This *non-* cares little about money.

Think and Write Write the Core Word that has the same prefix and base word as each noun below.

12. impossibility   13. irregularity   14. illiteracy   15. insecurity

WRITE ON YOUR OWN

Write a paragraph that compares and contrasts cats and dogs. Follow the writing process steps on pages 134–135 to write your paragraph. Use at least four Core Words from this lesson.

Prooofreding
  a   c
prakticee

1–5. Here is a draft of one student's paragraph. Find five misspelled Core Words and write them correctly.

Cats and dogs are as different as night and day. Cats are inndependent and impossible to train. Dogs are easy to train, but they do ilogical things like chasing cars. Cats sleep regularly and are nonvialent. Dogs, on the other hand, keep iregular hours and sometimes bite. When dogs get inpatient they bark, but cats meow and rub against things.

Now proofread your own paragraph and correct any errors.

CORE			CHALLENGE
illegible	impossible	independent	irresponsible
irrational	insecure	impatient	inconclusive
nonviolent	nonprofit	nonstandard	inescapable
illegal	impartial	incorrect	impersonal
irregular	illiterate	illogical	incapable

17 Spelling Astronomy Words

CORE

1. reentry
2. Uranus
3. Earth
4. astronaut
5. Mars
6. Venus
7. eclipse
8. Mercury
9. satellite
10. Pluto
11. Saturn
12. asteroid
13. Neptune
14. Jupiter
15. astronomer

CHALLENGE

16. weightlessness
17. Voyager
18. constellation
19. propellant
20. atmosphere

FOCUS

Sound	Spelling
/nep ′ tün/	Neptune
/vē ′nəs/	Venus

Say each word. Listen for familiar vowel sounds.

Study the spelling. Can you find familiar vowel spellings?

Write the words.

1–9. Write the Core Words that are proper nouns. Circle the letters that spell long vowel sounds.

10-12. Write the Core Words that start with **ast-**.

13–15. Write the remaining Core Words that are common nouns related to space. Circle the letters that spell long vowel sounds.

16–20. Write the Challenge Words. Circle any double consonants.

SPELLING TIP
Many astronomy words follow expected spellings.

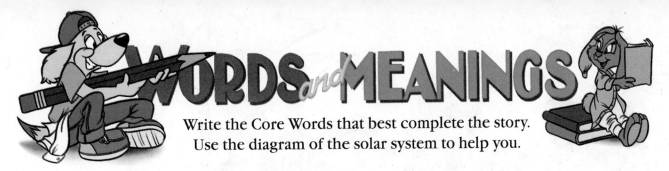

WORDS and MEANINGS

Write the Core Words that best complete the story.
Use the diagram of the solar system to help you.

FROM MARS TO PLUTO

In ancient times, people knew little about the universe. Now, thanks to powerful telescopes, an (1) can look at other galaxies. Scientists can even see the details of an (2) collision millions of miles away. During a total solar (3), they can closely view the sun's halo. Telescopes have also helped scientists learn about the planets and their positions in our solar system.

Closest to the sun is the small planet (4), followed by cloud-covered (5). Next in line is our own planet, (6). Just beyond our globe lies the red planet (7), which an (8) may visit someday. It could be many years, however, before a spacecraft can land there and then make a safe (9) into our atmosphere.

The fifth planet from the sun is giant (10). Next comes the planet (11), which is encircled by rings. More than one (12) orbits this planet, but its largest is called Titan. Seventh from the sun lies the planet (13), followed by the last large planet, (14). Finally, at the farthest reach of our solar system, lies tiny (15).

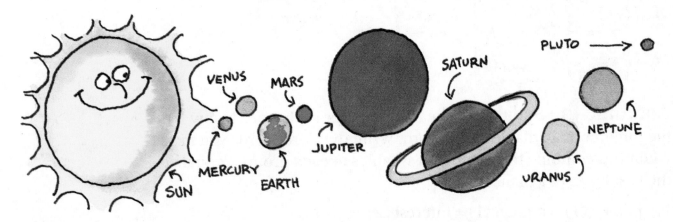

The Greek Word Part ast-

Many words that begin with *ast-* come from the Greek word *astron*, meaning "star." Match the words on the left with their meanings on the right. Write each word with its meaning.

16. asteroid
17. astronaut
18. astronomy

a person who flies in a spacecraft
the science that deals with heavenly bodies
a small rocky body that orbits the sun

Find the Secret Words

An *anagram* is a word or phrase made by changing the order of the letters in another word or phrase. Rearrange the letters in each message and write the Core Word you make. Capitalize the first letter of a planet name.

1. teen   pun
2. moon   starer
3. he   rat
4. a   roast   nut
5. my   curer

6. see   clip
7. teal   tiles
8. sun   tar
9. rams

Combine the Syllables

The number after each word below is the number of a syllable in the word. Write the Core Words you make when you combine the numbered syllables in each group. Capitalize the first letter of a planet name.

10. jubilee (1) + pigeon (1) + interest (2)
11. cereal (2) + envious (1) + geometry (4)
12. plural (1) + memento (3)
13. cameras (3) + terrific (1) + planetoid (3)
14. veranda (1) + alumnus (3)
15. graduate (2) + radio (1) + bonus (2)

Use the Dictionary

The words in a dictionary are given in alphabetical order. Rearrange the words below in alphabetical order. Check your answers in your Speller Dictionary.

16–20. Saturn, astronomer, astronaut, satellite, asteroid

Suppose that you could take a space journey anywhere within the solar system. Where would you go and what would you do? Write a poem about your imaginary trip into space. Use at least four Core Words from this lesson.

Proofreading praktice

1-4. Here is a draft of one student's poem. Find four misspelled Core Words and write them correctly.

If I could fly among the stars,
I'd go to Vennus and to Mars.
I'd make myself a satelite
And orbit them both day and night.
Compared to Pleuto they'd be hot,
And I the coolest astronot.

Now proofread your own poem and correct any errors.

CORE			CHALLENGE
reentry	Venus	Saturn	weightlessness
Uranus	eclipse	asteroid	Voyager
Earth	Mercury	Neptune	constellation
astronaut	satellite	Jupiter	propellant
Mars	Pluto	astronomer	atmosphere

Write a Core Word from Lesson 13 for each clue or definition below. Be careful. Each word can be easily misspelled.

1. a plant for flavoring food
2. something done to dough
3. a joint in the finger
4. a kind of fish

Write a Core Word from Lesson 14 that means the same as each underlined word below. Each word you write will have the ending *-ous*.

5. When she helped him up the stairs, I knew she was very <u>polite</u>.
6. His <u>funny</u> personality kept us amused.
7. Jack gets quite <u>jumpy</u> when flying in an airplane.
8. Dr. Joyce Simon is a <u>well-known</u> surgeon.

Rewrite the sentences or phrases below. Replace the underlined word or words with a Core Word from Lesson 15. Each word you write will have a /k/ sound. The corrected phrase or sentence is a famous quotation.

9. "What matters in a <u>personality</u> is not whether one holds this or that opinion: what matters is how proudly one upholds it."
    — GERMAINE DE STAEL

10. "<u>Method</u>! The very word is like the shriek of outraged Art."
    — LEONARD BACON

11. "The thing that numbs the heart is this: That men cannot devise Some <u>plan</u> of life to banish fear." — JAMES NORMAN HALL

12. "I am singing the best song ever was sung And it has a rousing <u>part that is repeated</u>." — HILAIRE BELLOC

REVIEW

Write a Core Word from Lesson 16 that means the opposite of each word or phrase below. Each word you write will have a negative prefix.

13. readable

14. accurate

15. prejudiced

16. makes money

Write a Core Word from Lesson 17 to complete each sentence below. Each word you write comes from the field of astronomy.

17. At nine o'clock we will witness a complete lunar ___.

18. As far as we know, ___ is the only planet where human beings live.

19. The launch of a new ___ will improve communications around the world.

20. The ___ gave a fascinating lecture about her recent discovery of a comet.

19 Spelling Words with the Suffix *-ity* or *-y*

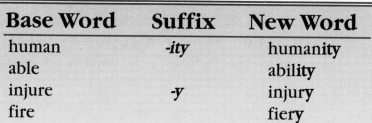

FOCUS

CORE

1. unity
2. popularity
3. ability
4. security
5. fiery
6. hostility
7. eternity
8. maturity
9. nationality
10. injury
11. humanity
12. slippery
13. majority
14. humidity
15. equality

CHALLENGE

16. probability
17. economy
18. formality
19. opportunity
20. neutrality

Base Word	Suffix	New Word
human	*-ity*	humanity
able		ability
injure	*-y*	injury
fire		fiery

Say each word. Listen for the suffix *-ity* or *-y*.

Study the spelling. Does the spelling of each base word change when the suffix is added? Does the meaning change?

Write the words.

1–6. Write the Core Words whose base words kept their spelling when *-ity* or *-y* was added.

7–15. Write the Core Words whose base words changed their spelling when *-ity* or *-y* was added.

16–20. Write the Challenge Words. Circle the suffix in each word.

SPELLING TIP
The spelling of a base word sometimes changes when the suffix *-ity* or *-y* is added.

WORDS and MEANINGS

Write the Core Words that best complete the story.

THE PATH TO NATIONALITY

In 1765 Great Britain ruled the American colonies. However, Britain's King George no longer enjoyed the (1) he had once had with his American subjects. He did not believe the colonists had the skill, or (2), to rule themselves.

When a stamp tax was imposed in 1765, some colonists would not pay. They made (3), furious speeches against British rule. They demanded, but were denied, (4) with British citizens in terms of voting rights.

In the heat and (5) of summer, the colonists' tempers flared. Many stated that they would rather give up their British (6) than be ruled by a heartless monarch for all (7). A sense of oneness, or (8), grew among them. The colonists felt that the king had done them a terrible (9).

Over the next decade, Great Britain imposed even harsher laws and taxes. King George sent troops overseas to provide (10) in case of uprisings. Colonists criticized the king's (11), dishonest nature and his lack of kindness, or (12). Soon the (13) of colonists foresaw war with Great Britain.

On April 19, 1775, open (14) broke out, and the first shots of the Revolutionary War were fired. That day, America began its journey from youth to (15).

The Prefix re-

The prefix **re-** adds the meaning "again" to a word. For example, *refresh* means "to make fresh again." Add **re-** to each word. Then write a short definition of the new word.

16. print
17. cycle
18. locate

19. assure
20. finish

Decode the Pictograms Write a Core Word for each pictogram.

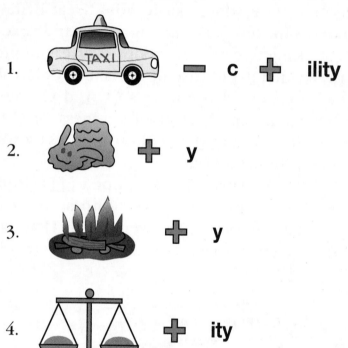

1. [TAXI] − c ➕ **ility**

2. 🪨 ➕ **y**

3. 🔥 ➕ **y**

4. ⚖ ➕ **ity**

Think and Write If a word is blue, write a Core Word that is a synonym for the word. If the word is red, write a Core Word that is an antonym for it.

5. friendliness
6. **wound**
7. youth
8. **timelessness**
9. **safety**

Search and Write Write Core Words to answer the questions.

10–12. Which three words have the long *u* sound in their first syllable?

13. Which word contains the /ôr/ sound you hear in *formal?*

14–15. Which two words have the short *a* sound in their third syllable?

Imagine that you are a colonist who wants American independence. Write a short speech persuading others to join your cause. Follow the writing process steps on pages 134–135 to write your speech. Use at least four Core Words from this lesson.

Proofreding praktice

1–4. Here is a draft of one student's speech. Find four misspelled Core Words and write them correctly.

It is time for all of us to stand up for equallity. We must not suffer any more injurey at the hands of the king. Instead we must come together in unity and let our firey spirits lead us. We have the ableity and maturity to be a great nation, so let us begin.

Now proofread your own speech and correct any errors.

CORE			CHALLENGE
unity	hostility	humanity	probability
popularity	eternity	slippery	economy
ability	maturity	majority	formality
security	nationality	humidity	opportunity
fiery	injury	equality	neutrality

20 Spelling Words with the Suffix -ment or -ness

FOCUS

CORE

1. refreshment
2. kindness
3. development
4. cleanliness
5. amusement
6. judgment
7. loneliness
8. agreement
9. measurement
10. cleverness
11. enchantment
12. equipment
13. foolishness
14. management
15. settlement

CHALLENGE

16. astonishment
17. encouragement
18. accomplishment
19. cautiousness
20. achievement

Base Word	Suffix	New Word
equip	-ment	equipment
judge		judgment
clever	-ness	cleverness
lonely		loneliness

Say each word. Listen for the suffix *-ment* or *-ness*.

Study the spelling. Does the spelling of each base word change when the suffix is added? Does the meaning change?

Write the words.

1–12. Write the Core Words whose base words keep their spelling when *-ment* or *-ness* is added.

13–15. Write the Core Words whose base-word spellings change when *-ment* or *-ness* is added.

16–20. Write the Challenge Words. Circle the suffix in each word.

SPELLING TIP
Most base words keep their spelling when the suffix *-ment* or *-ness* is added.

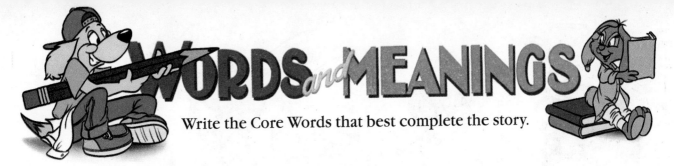
A SUPER AMUSEMENT PARK

If you are visiting Greenville, be sure to stop at Fun World, the giant (1) park. This park was under (2) for six years before it opened. The careful planning given to it shows up in every detail. The (3) used to operate the rides is inspected regularly. Most workers, even those at the top levels of (4), are in uniform. In the (5) of many, Fun World is America's best-run theme park.

Anyone entering the park will be struck by its (6), for not a speck of litter ruins the mood of magical (7). There are dozens of (8) stands for hungry tourists, who will never suffer from (9) thanks to the endless crowds. Theme areas like the pioneer (10) have been designed with great skill and (11). Clowns roam around, thrilling visitors with their tricks and silly (12).

Perhaps the only drawback to Fun World is its size: the park's overall (13) is 200 acres. After a day there, most tired tourists are in (14) that the park is BIG. However, the smiles and (15) of the staff make up for a few aches and pains.

More About the Noun Suffix -ness

The suffix -ness changes an adjective to a noun. When you add -ness to a word that ends in y, you must change the y to i. Add -ness to these words to create nouns. Write the new words.

16. fiery
17. lovely
18. sloppy
19. cloudy
20. lively
21. greedy
22. clumsy

Connect the Word Parts
Combine the syllables and suffixes to form six Core Words. You will need to use some syllables and suffixes more than once.

1-6.

clev · er · ment · de · vel · op · ness · a · muse · kind · agree · manage

Start, Skip, and Pass
Write the Core Word that fits each clue.

7. Start at the beginning, and you'll find *set*.
8. Skip the first letter, and you'll find *quip*.
9. Pass the first five letters, and you'll find *lines*.
10. Start at the beginning, and you'll find *lone*.
11. Skip the first two letters, and you'll find *chant*.
12. Pass the first two letters, and you'll find *fresh*.

Collect the Clowns
Figure out the missing letters and write the Core Words. Then use the letters that would go above the clown faces to write the answer to question 16.

13. _ _ o _ _ _ _ e _ _   15. _ u _ _ _ _ _ _

14. _ _ _ s _ _ _ _ _ n _

16. What do people have at theme parks?

Use the Dictionary
Look up the suffix of each word below in your Speller Dictionary. Write the first definition that is given for the suffix.

17. agreement   18. kindness   19. bearable   20. soloist

Write a paragraph describing your plan for the world's greatest theme park. Follow the writing process steps on pages 134–135 to write your description. Use at least four Core Words from this lesson.

Proofreading practice

1–4. Here is a draft of one student's description. Find four misspelled Core Words and write them correctly.

> My amusment park would be as big as a city. It would be free for everybody, and kids would take care of its management and cleanlyness. The park would have amazing equippment, such as a flying Ferris wheel and a roller coaster ride five miles long. I'd call the place Wonderland, and its main themes would be excitement and enchantmint.

Now proofread your own description and correct any errors.

CORE			CHALLENGE
refreshment	judgment	enchantment	astonishment
kindness	loneliness	equipment	encouragement
development	agreement	foolishness	accomplishment
cleanliness	measurement	management	cautiousness
amusement	cleverness	settlement	achievement

21 Spelling Words with the Prefix *in-* or *im-*

FOCUS

CORE

1. integrate
2. influence
3. immerse
4. inflate
5. instinct
6. inhale
7. impose
8. inspire
9. include
10. instruct
11. import
12. intrude
13. increase
14. involve
15. ingredient

CHALLENGE

16. investigate
17. indebted
18. institution
19. invasion
20. inhibit

Say each word. Listen for the prefix in the first syllable.

Study Which prefix is used in *inhale*, *inspire*, and *intrude*? Which prefix is used in *immerse* and in *import*? Do you always recognize the base word?

Write the words.

1–12. Write the Core Words that begin with the prefix *in-*.

13–15. Write the Core Words that begin with the prefix *im-*. Circle the letter that follows *im-*.

16–20. Write the Challenge Words. Circle the word in which *in-* is followed by a familiar base word.

SPELLING TIP
The prefixes *in-* and *im-* can mean "in," "into," "on," "within," or "toward." *Im-* is used instead of *in-* before words or roots that begin with *m* or *p*.

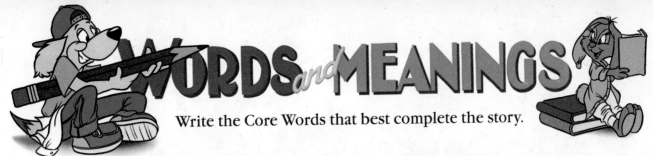

WORDS and MEANINGS

Write the Core Words that best complete the story.

A NATURAL BOND

Kelly feels that her grandfather had more (1) on her than anyone. Although he ran an (2) business for 45 years, his true love was always nature. He tried not to (3) his interests upon Kelly, but he would often (4) her on his walks in the woods. Together they would (5) the scent of the pines and agree there was no better smell.

As they walked, Kelly's grandfather would (6) her in the ways of nature. He pointed out small creatures and explained how (7) helped them survive. He showed her how not to (8) upon their territory and frighten them. He taught Kelly about odd plants like puffballs, which puff up, or (9), with powdery spores. Then they blow the spores out.

Her grandfather's teachings helped Kelly's knowledge of nature to (10). Walks in the woods became an essential (11) of her life, and she began to (12) herself in books about nature. Now Kelly plans to (13) herself in a career that will (14) her interest in science with her love of the outdoors. Meanwhile, the memory of her grandfather continues to guide and (15) her.

More About the Prefixes *in-* and *im-*

The prefixes *in-* and *im-* are also negative prefixes. When added to a base word, they create a new word that means the opposite of the base word. Use the *in-* or *im-* prefix to write words that mean the following.

16. not accurate
17. not movable
18. not visible
19. not practical
20. not direct

Get to the Roots
The word on each tree in the woods shares a root with a Core Word. Write the Core Word that has the same root as the tree word.

1–6.

(tree words: construction, excluding, protruded, revolving, composed, transpired)

Break the Code
Each letter of a Core Word is represented by a number. Use the code to write Core Words.

Code	1	2	3	4	5	6	7	8	9	10	11	12	13	14
Letter	c	d	e	f	g	i	l	m	n	p	r	s	t	u

7. 6 - 9 - 5 - 11 - 3 - 2 - 6 - 3 - 9 - 13
8. 6 - 9 - 12 - 13 - 6 - 9 - 1 - 13
9. 6 - 9 - 4 - 7 - 14 - 3 - 9 - 1 - 3
10. 6 - 8 - 8 - 3 - 11 - 12 - 3

Think and Write
Write Core Words to answer the questions.

11–13. Which three words spell the long *a* sound with *a-e*?
14–15. Which two words are pronounced differently when they are used as verbs and as nouns?

Use the Dictionary
Write each word given below and draw a line between the syllables. Then draw a double line under each stressed syllable. If a word has two stressed syllables, draw a single line under the syllable with the lesser stress. Check your answers in your Speller Dictionary.

<u>in</u>/flu/ence

16. inspire   17. inspiration   18. ingredient   19. integrate   20. integration

Write a paragraph describing a person who has had an important effect on your life. Follow the writing process steps on pages 134–135 to write your description. Use at least four Core Words from this lesson.

Proofreding praktice

1–4. Here is a draft of one student's description. Find four mispelled Core Words and write them correctly.

> My aunt Martha has had a big imfluence on my life. Like Martin Luther King, jr, she has worked to help intigrate schools and increese civil rights. Her words and actions never fail to enspire me

5–7. This student forgot to capitalize an abbreviation and left out two periods. Copy the description and correct the errors.

Now proofread your own description and correct any errors.

CORE			CHALLENGE
integrate	inhale	import	investigate
influence	impose	intrude	indebted
immerse	inspire	increase	institution
inflate	include	involve	invasion
instinct	instruct	ingredient	inhibit

22 Spelling Math Words

CORE

1. remainder
2. dividend
3. metric
4. addition
5. difference
6. subtraction
7. fraction
8. rectangle
9. geometry
10. division
11. perimeter
12. calculate
13. numerator
14. multiplication
15. quotient

Say each word. Listen for familiar vowel and consonant sounds.

Study the spelling. Can you find familiar vowel spellings? What other familiar spellings do you find? Do you see any unusual spellings?

Write the words.

1–11. Write the Core Words that have two or three syllables. Circle any spelling patterns that are unfamiliar to you.

12–15. Write the Core Words that have four or more syllables. Circle any spelling patterns that are unfamiliar to you.

16–20. Write the Challenge Words. Underline the word that has five syllables.

SPELLING TIP
Many math words follow expected spellings. Others have spellings that must be remembered.

CHALLENGE

16. trapezoid
17. denominator
18. rhombus
19. circumference
20. algebra

Words and Meanings

Write the Core Words that best complete the story.

COMPUTER GENIUS

Paulo has a new computer program that quickly performs the four basic number operations. In an instant it can give Paulo the sum of an (1) problem or the product of a (2) problem. When Paulo wants to find out the (3) between two numbers, he just tells the computer to do the (4). The program also does (5), Paulo's least favorite operation. Not only will the computer give Paulo the (6), but it will also tell him the (7)—the leftover number!

In a split second, Paulo's program can (8) the result of a problem such as 1,983 - 947. To solve a problem such as 120 ÷ 6, Paulo simply has to punch in the (9) of 120 and the divisor of 6. The computer does the rest, quickly coming up with the answer—20. It can take a (10) such as 8/10 and express it in lowest terms by dividing both the (11) and denominator by 2.

Paulo can also use the program to solve problems in (12). This is the branch of math that deals with angles and shapes. When given the lengths of the sides of a square or a (13), the program can find the length of the (14). All answers are given in (15) units of measurement.

120 ÷ 6 =
15 × 1/8 =
2967.543
× 7.614

The Latin Roots *frac* and *frag*

The roots *frac* and *frag* come from a Latin word meaning "to break." Write the word that fits each meaning below.

fraction	fragile	refraction
fracture	fragment	

16. easily broken
17. the bending of light waves
18. a number such as 1/2

19. to crack or break
20. a part that is broken off

Be a Math Whiz Study the chalkboard. Then write Core Words to complete the exercises.

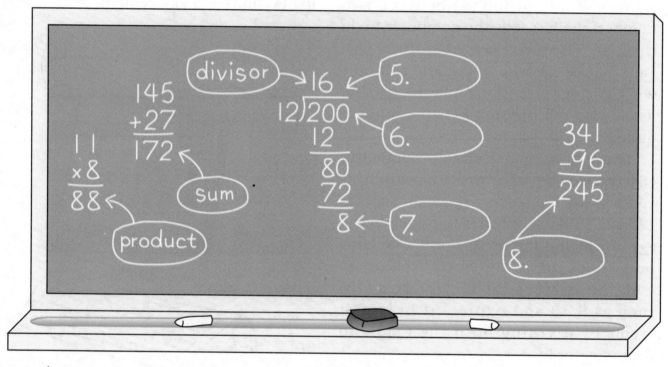

1–4. Write the name of the number operation shown in each problem on the chalkboard. Work from left to right.

5–8. Write the Core Words that are missing from the labels numbered 5–8. Use four different Core Words.

Search and Write Write the Core Words that fit the clues.

9–11. They end with the /ər/ sound.

12. It has the long *e* sound in its first and last syllables.

13. It contains the letters *ng*.

14. It has two /k/ sounds, both spelled with *c*.

15. It ends with the suffix *-ic.*

16. Its second syllable is the suffix *-ion.*

You often use math without realizing it. Write a paragraph that explains how you use math every day. Follow the steps of the writing process on pages 134–135 to write your paragraph. Use at least four Core Words from this lesson.

Proofreding prakticee

1–4. Here is a draft of one student's paragraph. Find four misspelled Core Words and write them correctly.

> I love math because it's clear and simple, which is a big differense from other subjects. When you work out an adition or subtraction problem, there can be only one right answer. The same is true for multaplication and division problems. If you get a wrong answer, you just calkulate the problem again until it comes out right.

Now proofread your own paragraph and correct any errors.

CORE			CHALLENGE
remainder	subtraction	perimeter	trapezoid
dividend	fraction	calculate	denominator
metric	rectangle	numerator	rhombus
addition	geometry	multiplication	circumference
difference	division	quotient	algebra

23 Spelling the Names of Countries

FOCUS

CORE

1. Switzerland
2. Argentina
3. Germany
4. Zambia
5. Israel
6. Canada
7. Botswana
8. Great Britain
9. Belgium
10. Vietnam
11. Ireland
12. Pakistan
13. Thailand
14. Mexico
15. Brazil

Say each word. Listen for familiar vowel and consonant sounds.

Study the spelling. Can you find familiar vowel spellings? What other familiar spellings do you find? How does each word begin? Are there any unusual spellings?

Write the words.

1–15. Write the Core Words in alphabetical order. Circle any unusual spellings.

16–20. Write the Challenge Words in alphabetical order. Underline the word that has a double consonant.

SPELLING TIP
Many country names follow expected spellings. Others have spellings that must be remembered. Always capitalize the names of countries.

CHALLENGE

16. Venezuela
17. Egypt
18. Philippines
19. Uruguay
20. Ecuador

WORDS and MEANINGS

Write the Core Words that best complete the story.

Around the World in Eighty Ways

Come join Round-the-World Tours for a whirlwind trip around the globe! Our first stops will be in North America. Here, during a brief visit in (1), we will meet some Mounties. Then we will fly down to Acapulco, (2), for a grand fiesta.

Next, we are off to South America. What fun it will be to see a soccer game in Buenos Aires, the capital of (3)! Then we'll head for (4), the continent's largest country, and take an exciting trip down the Amazon.

Our next destination will be Africa. Here you will watch native dances in (5) and learn Botswanan customs as you travel through (6).

When the tour arrives in Europe, you can visit the Black Forest in (7) and climb the Alps in (8). You can buy a handknit sweater in Dublin, (9), and Belgian lace in (10). In (11) you will see the famous Tower of London.

Then we'll head into Asia, making a quick stop in (12) to relax on the beautiful Tel Aviv beaches. We'll go from there to (13), where you'll find many treasures in the Pakistani bazaars. When we get to (14), we will sample some wonderful Vietnamese foods. Finally, in (15), you may want to visit some Thai temples.

Forming Proper Adjectives

Follow the directions to turn each proper noun into a proper adjective.

16. Iraq + i
17. Norway - ay + egian
18. Japan + ese
19. Turkey - ey + ish
20. Peru + vian

Find the Origin
The names of eight items on the menu below originate from Core Words. Write the Core Words.

1–8.

GLOBE CAFE: TODAY'S SPECIALS

Breakfast
Belgian waffles with
Canadian maple syrup $3.95

Lunch
Swiss cheese on rye $3.50

Dinner
Mexican taco salad $6.95
Spicy Thai chicken $7.50
German sauerkraut $3.50
Irish soda bread $1.95

Drinks

Brazilian
cocoa
$2.25

Match Flags and Countries
Write the Core Word that names the country represented by each flag. Use the letter clues to help you.

9.

G _ _ _ _   _ _ t _ _ _

11.

V _ _ _ _ _ _

10.

Z _ _ _ _ _

12.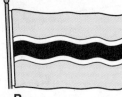

B _ _ _ _ _ _ _

Use Names to Name Countries
Each underlined name in these sentences can be found in a Core Word. Write the Core Words.

13. Did <u>Rae</u> go with you to the Middle East?
14. Did <u>Stan</u> buy a rug on his trip to Asia?
15. In which South American country did you run into <u>Tina</u>?

Make a list of the countries you would like most to visit. Next to each country name, note what you are most interested in seeing there. Use at least four Core Words from this lesson.

THAILAND 4,500 MI
BOTSWANA 8,600 MI
IRELAND 2,700 MI
MEXICO 11,000 MI
PAKISTAN 9,400 MI

Prooofreding prakticee

a — c

1-4. Here is a draft of one student's list. Find four misspelled Core Words and write them correctly.

> *I would like to visit:*
> *—Mexaco, to see the Mayan ruins*
> *—Brazill, to see the rain forests*
> *—Botswana, to see a diamond mine*
> *—Switserland, to see the Alps*
> *—Tailand, to see its temples*

Now proofread your own list and correct any errors.

CORE			CHALLENGE
Switzerland	Canada	Ireland	Venezuela
Argentina	Botswana	Pakistan	Egypt
Germany	Great Britain	Thailand	Philippines
Zambia	Belgium	Mexico	Uruguay
Israel	Vietnam	Brazil	Ecuador

Write the Core Word from Lesson 19 that is the synonym of each word below.

1. safety
2. dampness
3. wound
4. togetherness

Write each phrase or sentence below. Replace the underlined word or words with a Core Word from Lesson 20. Each word will end with **-ness** or **-ment**. The corrected phrase or sentence is a famous quotation.

5. "Niceness and generosity...form the true morality of human actions."
   — GERMAINE DE STAËL

6. "I grow lean in the state of being alone and unhappy, like a water lily gnawed by a beetle."
   — KACCIPĒTTU NANNĀKAIYĀR (3rd Century Indian woman)

7. "I care not who knows it—I write for the general state of being entertained." — SIR WALTER SCOTT

8. " 'Tis distance lends magic to the view." — THOMAS CAMPBELL

Write a Core Word you have studied in Lesson 21 to complete each sentence. Each word will begin with **im-** or **in-**.

9. If you ___ the balloon too much, it will pop.
10. It is against the law to ___ products from certain countries.
11. If you ___ a cold glass in hot water, it may crack.
12. When Maija had a bad cough, the doctor told her to ___ a special vapor.

Write a Core Word you studied in Lesson 22 for each clue below. Each word will be related to mathematics.

13. One-third for example.
14. The top number in number 1/3.
15. It goes with addition, subtraction, and division.
16. The answer to a division problem.

Write a Core Word from Lesson 23 using these clues. Each word is the name of a country.

17. A middle eastern country. It starts with *I*.
18. A country in Africa. It begins with *B*.
19. A European country. It begins with *B*.
20. A Southeast Asian country. It begins with *V*.

25 Spelling Words with the Suffix -ion

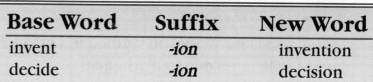

CORE

1. possession
2. decision
3. vegetation
4. depression
5. occupation
6. invention
7. reaction
8. satisfaction
9. admission
10. disposition
11. suspension
12. absorption
13. definition
14. digestion
15. permission

CHALLENGE

16. concession
17. recommendation
18. interruption
19. extension
20. cooperation

Base Word	Suffix	New Word
invent	*-ion*	invention
decide	*-ion*	decision

Say each word. Listen for the suffix in the final syllable.

Study the spelling. Can you find familiar base words and a suffix? How is the suffix spelled? Does the spelling of the base word sometimes change when the suffix is added? Does the meaning change?

Write the words.

   1–5. Write the Core Words whose base words keep their spelling when *-ion* is added.

  6–15. Write the Core Words whose base words change their spelling when *-ion* is added.

16–20. Write the Challenge Words. Circle any double consonants or double vowels.

SPELLING TIP
The spelling of a base word sometimes changes when *-ion* is added.

Write the Core Words that best complete the story.

THE BEAT GOES ON

I was thrilled that Judy had asked me to play drums in her band. When Mom and Dad gave me (1) to do it, my immediate (2) was to jump for joy. Then I rushed my drum set, my prized (3), over to Judy's and set it up on the stage in the garage.

At that first practice, my (4) in the music was so deep that I forgot to look around me. Suddenly, I began to fall backwards off the stage. I guess I hit my head, and everything went black. When I woke up I was in a hospital bed with my leg hanging in (5).

Now I usually have a cheerful (6), but the sight of that cast sent me into a deep (7). The doctor came in and announced her (8) that my (9) as a drummer would be on hold for a while. After I asked a few more questions, she finally made the (10) that I'd be in the hospital for a week. I groaned, thinking of a whole week of hospital food that didn't agree with my (11).

Before long I had used my powers of (12) to turn my fate around. Beating on the cast with my drumsticks, I managed to get in a lot of practice that week. Plus it gave me a sense of (13). It was certainly better than staring out the window at the (14)! Maybe that's the (15) of a true drummer—someone who can find the beat anywhere.

The Noun Suffix *-ion*

The suffix *-ion* is used to form nouns from verbs. It means "the act of," "the state of being," or "the result of." Write the word that fits each meaning below.

16. the act of instructing
17. the act of contributing
18. the act of opposing

Drum Up Some Answers Study the letters on the drum. Then make five different Core Words from those letters. You may use any letter more than once to make a word, but you may not add letters to the drum. Write the Core Words.

1–5.

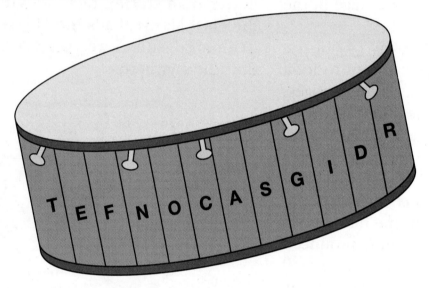

Think and Write Write the Core Word that completes each statement.

6. *Aircraft* is to *jet* as *bridge* is to ___.
7. *Happy* is to *mood* as *cheerful* is to ___.
8. *Smile* is to *frown* as *happiness* is to ___.
9. *Artist* is to *art* as *inventor* is to ___.

Search and Write Write Core Words to answer the questions.

10–11. Which four-syllable words have the long *a* sound in their third syllable?
   12. Which word contains the /ôr/ sound spelled *or*?
13–14. Which two words contain a smaller word that means "a job with a special purpose"?
   15. In which word is the /z/ sound spelled with *ss*?

WRITE ON YOUR OWN

Write a letter in which you apply for the job of your dreams.
Follow the writing process steps on pages 134–135 to write
your letter. Use at least four Core Words from this lesson.

Proofreading practice

1–4. Here is a draft of one student's letter. Find four misspelled
Core Words and write them correctly.

March 12, 1996

Dear Mr. Rockinroll:

With your permision, I would like to be a guitarist
in your band. I am well suited for this occupasion. I
have an electric guitar in my possetion, and I can
play any song to your satisfaction. Isn't hiring me
the right decizion?

Sincerely,

Amy Stringer

Now proofread your own letter and correct any errors.

CORE			CHALLENGE
possession	invention	suspension	concession
decision	reaction	absorption	recommendation
vegetation	satisfaction	definition	interruption
depression	admission	digestion	extension
occupation	disposition	permission	cooperation

26 Spelling Words with the Suffix -ance or -ence

FOCUS

CORE

1. patience
2. abundance
3. reluctance
4. experience
5. defiance
6. allowance
7. dependence
8. distance
9. annoyance
10. resistance
11. violence
12. disturbance
13. endurance
14. convenience
15. guidance

CHALLENGE

16. compliance
17. appearance
18. intelligence
19. consequence
20. acquaintance

Base Word	Suffix	New Word
allow	-ance	allowance
patient	-ence	patience

Say each word. Listen for the suffix in the final syllable.

Study the spelling. Can you find familiar base words and suffixes? How is the suffix spelled? Does the spelling of the base word sometimes change when the suffix is added? Does the meaning change?

Write the words.

1–10. Write the Core Words with the **-ance** suffix.

11–15. Write the Core Words with the **-ence** suffix.

16–20. Write the Challenge Words. Circle the suffix. Underline any words or word parts you recognize.

SPELLING TIP

The spelling of a base word sometimes changes when **-ance** or **-ence** is added.

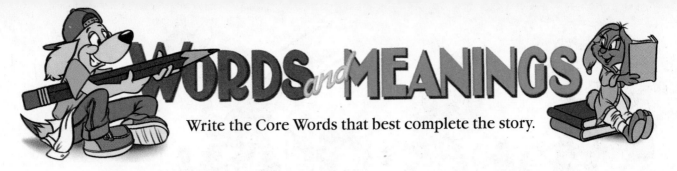

WORDS and MEANINGS

Write the Core Words that best complete the story.

UPHOLDERS OF THE LAW

Many law officers show a (1) to discuss their work. Anyone who has had (2) with police work, however, knows that it is a demanding job.

Police officers must have the physical (3) to spend long hours on the beat. Some travel a great (4) on foot, without the (5) of a squad car. Law officers also must fill out an (6) of paperwork and not complain that it is an (7). No matter how tired they are, they must keep their (8) with the public. This is because our (9) on them in emergencies is total.

When someone creates a (10) of the peace, the police must offer advice and (11). Many officers will try to make an (12) for simple thoughtlessness. But when there is willful (13) of the law, or when someone shows (14) to obeying them, police must act firmly. After all, their job is to prevent dangerous acts of (15) from occurring.

Synonyms

Write the Core Word that has the same meaning as each word below.

16. plenty
17. bother
18. hesitation

19. direction
20. remoteness

Locate the Police Cars

Each capital letter and number is the location of a police car on the city grid. For example, D4 (row D, column 4) is the location of car *b*. Find all the cars in each group. Use the letters on the cars to write a Core Word.

1. <u>A1</u> <u>E4</u> <u>D5</u> <u>A2</u> <u>D1</u> <u>C1</u> <u>B3</u> <u>D1</u>
2. <u>E4</u> <u>C1</u> <u>C1</u> <u>B2</u> <u>A4</u> <u>E4</u> <u>C1</u> <u>B3</u> <u>D1</u>
3. <u>C5</u> <u>D1</u> <u>E3</u> <u>A2</u> <u>E3</u> <u>D5</u> <u>E4</u> <u>C1</u> <u>B3</u> <u>D1</u>
4. <u>B5</u> <u>D1</u> <u>A1</u> <u>D1</u> <u>C1</u> <u>B5</u> <u>D1</u> <u>C1</u> <u>B3</u> <u>D1</u>
5. <u>E4</u> <u>D4</u> <u>E2</u> <u>C1</u> <u>B5</u> <u>E4</u> <u>C1</u> <u>B3</u> <u>D1</u>
6. <u>C5</u> <u>D1</u> <u>C3</u> <u>E2</u> <u>B3</u> <u>D5</u> <u>E4</u> <u>C1</u> <u>B3</u> <u>D1</u>

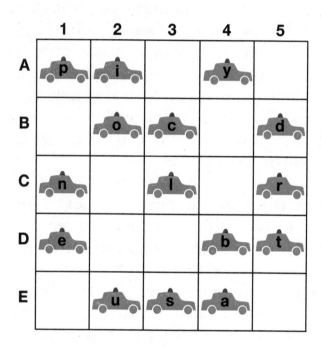

Finish the Phrases

Write the Core Word that best completes each familiar phrase.

7. a ___ store
8. no substitute for ___
9. keep your ___
10. a ___ counselor
11. in ___ of authority
12. a ___ of the peace

Get to the Core

Write the Core Words that fit the clues.

13–14. These two words spell the long *i* sound in the same way.
15. This word is a synonym for *stamina*.
16. This word has the /ou/ sound in its second syllable.

Use the Dictionary

Look up each underlined Core Word in your Speller Dictionary. Write the definition that shows how the word is used in the sentence.

17. We got an <u>allowance</u> on the price of the TV because it was dented.
18. What chores do you have to do to earn your <u>allowance</u>?
19. The modern <u>convenience</u> I like best is the microwave oven.
20. Benches are provided for the <u>convenience</u> of park users.

Write a police report about a store robbery. Follow the writing process steps on pages 134–135 to write your report. Use at least four Core Words from this lesson.

Proofreding prakticee

1-5. Here is a draft of one student's police report. Find five misspelled Core Words and write them correctly.

2:41 a.m.

The station received a call about a disturbence at the Handi-Mart conveniense store. Two officers drove the four-mile distants and found a robbery in progress. A suspect was captured after offering no resistence. The officers handcuffed the suspect and avoided violense.

Now proofread your own police report and correct any errors.

CORE			CHALLENGE
patience	allowance	violence	compliance
abundance	dependence	disturbance	appearance
reluctance	distance	endurance	intelligence
experience	annoyance	convenience	consequence
defiance	resistance	guidance	acquaintance

27 Spelling Words with the Prefix *pre-* or *pro-*

CORE

1. preview
2. propose
3. prearrange
4. prehistoric
5. proclamation
6. predict
7. progress
8. premature
9. preparation
10. provoke
11. precaution
12. projection
13. preface
14. prefix
15. procedure

CHALLENGE

16. precedent
17. procession
18. prescribe
19. preoccupied
20. premonition

Say each word. Listen for the prefix in the first syllable.

Study the spelling. Can you always find familiar base words and prefixes? How is the prefix spelled in *premature?* How is the prefix spelled in *progress?* How does the prefix affect the meaning of each word?

Write the words.

1–9. Write the Core Words that begin with the prefix **pre-**.

10–15. Write the Core Words that begin with the prefix **pro-**.

16–20. Write the Challenge Words. Circle the prefix in each word.

SPELLING TIP

The prefix **pre-** means "before or ahead of time." The prefix **pro-** means "forward," "forth," or "out." Prefixes may be combined with a base word or a word part called a root.

WORDS and MEANINGS

Write the Core Words that best complete the story.

A PREHISTORIC RECORD

Some animals and plants that lived ages ago, in (1) times, have left their remains behind. These remains are called *fossils.* No one can foretell, or (2), exactly where they can be found. However, some areas are richer in fossils than others.

When scientists choose a dig site, there must be a great deal of (3) before they begin work. They must (4) the organization of the dig. They must map out exactly where they (5) to dig and what the step-by-step (6) will be. Since many fossils are found in deserts or deep canyons, scientists must take every (7) against a harsh climate or accidental falls.

They often dig in hard-to-reach spots, such as a rocky (8), so (9) may be slow.

If scientists find old bones that arouse or (10) their interest, they must be sure not to make (11) judgments about what the bones may be. Once they identify the fossils, they can give them a scientific name. Often these have a Greek or Latin (12) such as **stego-** or **ptero-**. Many scientists then give other scientists a (13) of their finds in a scientific journal. After that a general (14) about the discovery is made to the public. The discovery may even be noted in the (15) to a book about fossil hunting.

The Suffix *-ic*

The suffix *-ic* means "having to do with" or "like." For example, *prehistoric* means "having to do with prehistory." Write a definition of each word below. Use "having to do with" or "like" in your definition.

16. meteoric
17. athletic
18. economic
19. nomadic
20. volcanic

Word Play

Sort and Spell Assemble these fossil fragments to form four Core Words. Write the words. You will need to use each prefix twice.

1–4.

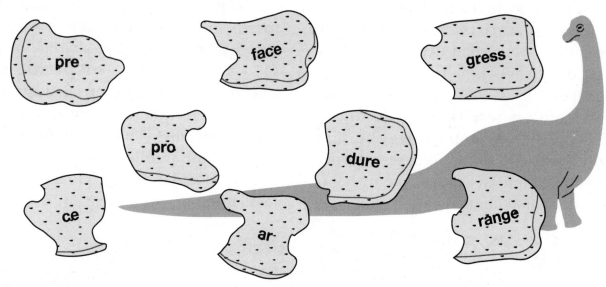

pre face gress pro dure ce ar range

Recall the Words Write a Core Word that begins with **pre-** or **pro-** and matches each clue.

5. This **pre-** is always early for everything.
6. This **pro-** enjoys suggesting things.
7. This **pre-** attaches itself to the beginnings of words.
8. This **pre-** is always careful.
9. This **pro-** makes public announcements.
10. This **pre-** likes to see things before others do.

Jump Back and Spell Replace each letter below with the letter of the alphabet that comes before it. For example, replace *b* with *a, c* with *b,* and so on. Write the Core Words you find.

11. qspwplf
12. qsfijtupsjd
13. qspkfdujpo
14. qsfejdu
15. qsfqbsbujpo

Imagine that you are a scientist who has dug up the bones of a new kind of dinosaur. Write a journal entry about your discovery. Use at least four Core Words from this lesson.

DINOSAURS: WHAT HAPPENED?

Proofreading praktice

1–4. Here is a draft of one student's journal entry. Find four misspelled Core Words and write them correctly.

> March 2, 1999 How amazing. Today I made great progres. While digging in Flagstaff Arizona, I uncovered the bones of a prehistoric dinosaur. I may be primature in saying so, but I believe that this creature was the biggest to ever walk the earth. I perdict that my find will prevoke an outcry.

5–6. This student used one incorrect end punctuation mark and left out a comma between a city and state. Copy the journal entry and correct the errors.

Now proofread your own journal entry and correct any errors.

CORE			CHALLENGE
preview	predict	precaution	precedent
propose	progress	projection	procession
prearrange	premature	preface	prescribe
prehistoric	preparation	prefix	preoccupied
proclamation	provoke	procedure	premonition

28 Easily Misspelled Words

CORE

1. terrific
2. colonel
3. weird
4. sergeant
5. desert
6. dessert
7. occasion
8. thorough
9. yacht
10. embarrass
11. sheriff
12. cough
13. scissors
14. occurrence
15. soldier

CHALLENGE

16. aquarium
17. moccasin
18. gauge
19. accidentally
20. broccoli

Say each word. Listen for the vowel and consonant sounds.

Study the spelling. What tricky or unusual spelling patterns do you see?

Write the words.

1-3. Write the Core Words that have one syllable. Circle any unusual spellings you find.

4-11. Write the Core Words that have two syllables. Circle any unusual spellings you find.

12-15. Write the Core Words that have three syllables. Circle the double consonants and any unusual spellings you find.

16-20. Write the Challenge Words. Circle any unusual spellings you find.

SPELLING TIP
Some words are easily misspelled. You must find strategies to remember their unexpected spellings.

WORDS and MEANINGS

Write the Core Words that best complete the story.

A DESERT DIARY

I have been appointed the new (1) of Boomtown and am heading there. The country is dangerous, so I am traveling with two military officers, a (2) and a (3). They have ordered a (4) under their command to scout for water in this endless (5). The sun's (6) heat is scorching us, and our canteens are nearly empty. I fear that this may be the last (7) when I have strength enough to write.

Earlier today I experienced an odd (8). My parched throat was making me (9), so I drank my last drop of water. Suddenly a huge lake shimmered in front of me. The next moment I saw a huge (10) sailing across the sky. I cried out with joy, but they were only mirages. Boy, did I (11) myself by shouting about these strange, (12) visions!

Even as I write, my companions are conducting a very (13) search for cactuses. They will use (14) to cut open the plants. If we are lucky, there will be water inside. Surely no (15) could taste more delicious than this precious liquid!

Homophones

Homophones sound alike but have different spellings and meanings. Write the homophones in the order that matches each set of definitions.

kernel/colonel	desert/dessert
course/coarse	altar/alter
stationery/stationary	

16. writing paper; immovable
17. an army officer; a grain of corn
18. to change; a table in a house of worship
19. to abandon; an end-of-meal treat
20. rough; a series of classes

Round Up the Words
Write one or more Core Words that have the double consonants named in each sign.

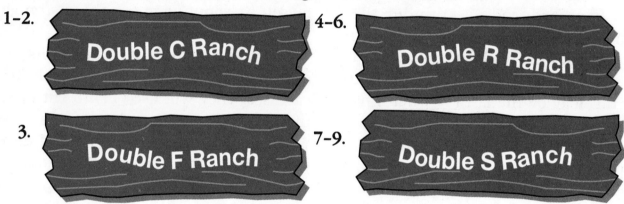

1–2.   **Double C Ranch**

4–6.   **Double R Ranch**

3.   **Double F Ranch**

7–9.   **Double S Ranch**

Take Time to Rhyme
Write the Core Word that creates a rhyme.

10. a small donkey that eats all its hay: a ___ burro
11. a place for parking a pleasure boat: a ___ spot
12. strange-looking facial hair: a ___ beard
13. a sickness pigs catch from their food bin: a trough ___
14. the diary of a military officer: a ___ journal

Say and Spell
Write the Core Words that contain the following spellings.

15. the /j/ sound spelled *di*
16. the /är/ sound spelled *er*
17. the /s/ sound spelled *sc*
18. the /z/ sound spelled *s*

Use the Dictionary
The words below are homographs. Homographs have the same spelling but different meanings and origins. Use your Speller Dictionary to look up the first listed meaning of each homograph below. Write the meaning.

19. desert[1]   20. desert[2]   21. graze[1]   22. graze[2]

Write an ending for the Desert Diary. Follow the writing process steps on pages 134–135 to write your story ending. Use at least four Core Words from this lesson.

Prooofreding prakticee

1-4. Here is a draft of one student's story ending. Find four misspelled Core Words and write them correctly.

> The sarjent and curnel have just returned with good news. They discovered a water hole in the dessert. The water they carried back has cured my cough. It looks like I'll get to be Boomtown's sheriff after all! I wish I could thank these men for saving my life, but it would embarass them.

Now proofread your own story ending and correct any errors.

CORE			CHALLENGE
terrific	dessert	sheriff	aquarium
colonel	occasion	cough	moccasin
weird	thorough	scissors	gauge
sergeant	yacht	occurrence	accidentally
desert	embarrass	soldier	broccoli

29 Spelling Words with Number Prefixes

CORE

1. universe
2. biceps
3. triplets
4. monotone
5. uniform
6. triangle
7. binoculars
8. monopoly
9. tricycle
10. unicorn
11. biannual
12. triplicate
13. unison
14. monorail
15. unicycle

CHALLENGE

16. triangular
17. bicentennial
18. unique
19. tripod
20. monopolize

Word	Meaning
monotone	one tone
biannual	twice a year
triangle	three sides
unicycle	one wheel

Say each word. Listen for the prefix in the first syllable.

Study the spelling. Can you find familiar base words? What prefixes do you find? What meaning does each prefix seem to have?

Write the words.

1–15. Write these headings across your paper: *bi-, mono-, tri-, uni-*. Under each heading write the Core Words that begin with that prefix.

16–20. Write the Challenge Words. Circle the prefix in each word.

SPELLING TIP
Some words that begin with
bi-, mono-, tri-, or *uni-*
have familiar base words. These prefixes
have numerical meanings.

WORDS and MEANINGS

Write the Core Words that best complete the story.

THE GREATEST CIRCUS IN THE UNIVERSE

Leo's Traveling Circus was making its (1) visit to town, and everyone planned to go. Because Leo's was the only circus that came to the area, it held a local (2) on circus entertainment. Nobody minded, though, because Leo's shows were always great.

Stepping into the big tent was like entering a magical (3). Leo, the ringmaster, stood in the center, wearing a spangled (4) and top hat. A bear rode around on the single wheel of a (5). Lions roared from cages on a small train that ran on a (6). Three clowns, dressed identically to look like (7), circled the ring on a three-person bike. Imagine! Instead of appearing in duplicate, they appeared in (8)! Another clown, dressed like a baby, rode around on a (9) with three huge wheels. A woman balanced on the shoulders of two other acrobats to form a human (10). A strong man bent a steel bar, showing off his (11).

For the finale, Leo announced in a loud, (12) voice that the world's only (13) would trot around the ring. The people far back in the stands peered through (14) to see the creature's gleaming horn. As the show ended, the audience clapped and cheered in (15).

Using Number Prefixes
Three number prefixes are given on the left. Add the prefixes to the words on the right to make new words that fit the definitions.

mono- = single	monthly
bi- = two	color
tri- = three	plane

16. having three colors
17. a plane with a single pair of wings
18. happening every two months

Search the Tent

Find the eight Core Words that are hidden in the puzzle on this circus tent. They are written across or down. Write the words on a separate piece of paper.

1–8.

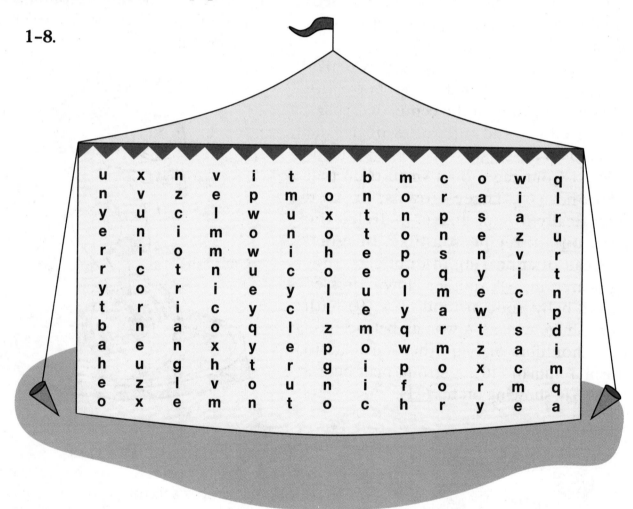

```
u  x  n  v  i  t  l  b  m  c  o  w  q
n  v  z  e  p  m  o  n  o  r  a  i  l
y  u  c  l  w  u  x  t  n  p  s  a  r
e  n  i  m  o  w  o  e  o  n  e  z  u
r  i  o  m  w  n  h  e  p  s  n  v  r
r  c  t  n  u  i  o  u  o  q  y  i  t
y  o  r  i  e  c  l  e  l  m  e  c  n
t  r  i  c  y  y  l  m  y  a  w  l  p
b  n  a  o  q  c  z  o  q  r  t  s  d
a  e  n  x  y  l  p  i  w  m  z  a  i
h  u  g  h  t  e  g  i  p  o  x  c  m
e  z  l  v  o  r  n  c  f  o  r  m  q
o  x  e  m  n  u  o  c  h  r  y  e  a
```

Match the Syllables

Write the Core Word that contains the syllable underlined in each word below.

9. in<u>tri</u>cate
10. coup<u>let</u>s
11. mo<u>lars</u>
12. tri<u>ceps</u>
13. per<u>son</u>al
14. con<u>verse</u>
15. nu<u>clear</u>

Imagine that you are a ticket seller for Leo's Traveling Circus. Write the sales pitch you would use to persuade people to see the show. Follow the writing process steps on pages 134–135 to write your sales pitch. Use at least four Core Words from this lesson.

Proofreading practice

1–5. Here is a draft of one student's sales pitch. Find five misspelled Core Words and write them correctly.

> Step right up, folks, and buy your tickets to Leo's Traveling Circus. You won't believe your eyes! You'll see triplits doing triplicate stunts on the trapeze. You'll gasp in unisson as an elephant rides a trycycle. You'll see the last unicorn in the univirse. So hurry on into the big top, where Leo has a monopolly on fun!

Now proofread your own sales pitch and correct any errors.

CORE			CHALLENGE
universe	triangle	biannual	triangular
biceps	binoculars	triplicate	bicentennial
triplets	monopoly	unison	unique
monotone	tricycle	monorail	tripod
uniform	unicorn	unicycle	monopolize

Write the Core Word from Lesson 25 that means the same as the word or phrase below. Each word has the suffix *-ion*.

1. job
2. something owned
3. sadness
4. meaning of a word

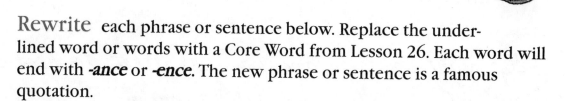

Rewrite each phrase or sentence below. Replace the underlined word or words with a Core Word from Lesson 26. Each word will end with *-ance* or *-ence*. The new phrase or sentence is a famous quotation.

5. "I can give you no better counsel than to endure with <u>the state of putting up with problems calmly</u>."—*OLIMPIA MORATA*

6. "... I believe one half of the world is born for the <u>comfort or advantage</u> of the other half..."—*SARAH SIDDONS*

7. "Facts were never pleasing to him. He acquired them with <u>unwillingness</u> and got rid of them with relief."—*SIR JAMES MATTHEW BARRIE*

8. "Sweetest melodies are those that are by <u>the fact of being far away</u> made more sweet."—*WILLIAM WORDSWORTH*

Write a Core Word from Lesson 27 that means the opposite of each word or phrase below. Each word will begin with *pro-* or *pre-*.

9. suffix
10. make calm
11. modern
12. move backward

Write a Core Word from Lesson 28 to complete each sentence below. The missing word will rhyme with the underlined word.

13. An army officer's magazine is a ___ journal.
14. A burning boat is a hot ___.
15. Strange facial hair is a ___ beard.
16. An injured cookie is a hurt ___.

Write a Core Word from Lesson 29 to complete each sentence below. Each word will begin with *bi-*, *mono-*, *tri-*, or *uni-*.

17. The child rode her three-wheeled ___ down the sidewalk.
18. Jenna stared through the ___ at the soaring hawk.
19. Black ink stained the pocket of the nurse's white ___.
20. If you give a speech in a dull ___, your audience may fall asleep.

31 Spelling Words with the -ive Suffix

FOCUS

CORE

1. exclusive
2. active
3. protective
4. destructive
5. creative
6. informative
7. captive
8. aggressive
9. detective
10. expressive
11. comparative
12. defensive
13. alternative
14. conclusive
15. defective

CHALLENGE

16. cooperative
17. abrasive
18. cumulative
19. descriptive
20. communicative

Base Word	Suffix	New Word
act	*-ive*	active
create	*-ive*	creative
inform	*-ive*	informative

Say each word. Listen for the suffix in the final syllable.

Study the spelling. How is the suffix spelled? Does the spelling of a base word ever change when the suffix is added? How does the suffix change the meaning of the word?

Write the words.

   1–6. Write the Core Words in which the base word does not change when *-ive* is added.
   7–15. Write the Core Words whose base words change when *-ive* is added.
   16–20. Write the Challenge Words. Circle the suffix in each word.

SPELLING TIP
The spelling of a base word sometimes changes when *-ive* is added.

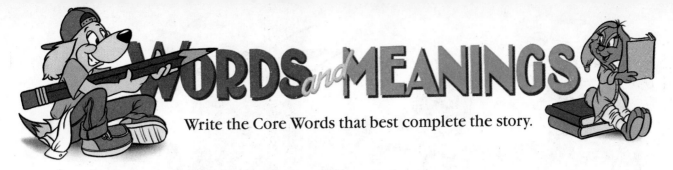

WORDS and MEANINGS

Write the Core Words that best complete the story.

NADER THE CRUSADER

Some years ago Ralph Nader wrote an article called "The *Safe* Car You Can't Buy." His article was fact-filled and (1). He claimed to have (2) evidence proving that most cars were unsafe. It stated that the auto industry's only, or (3), concern was making stylish cars. The industry spent millions on imaginative and (4) car designs but ignored safety features.

Automakers went on the (5) after the article appeared. People began to demand an (6) to unsafe cars. They refused to be treated as (7) buyers any longer. Auto companies began to include (8) devices such as seatbelts in their cars. These helped reduce the (9) effects of accidents.

Today Nader continues his role as a consumer (10). He and his organization look for flawed or (11) products. His lively and (12) face has appeared often on TV, where he has reported on (13) features and pricing of a number of products. Some people feel Nader is too (14). Nevertheless, most people expect Nader to be (15) for many years to come.

Antonyms

An antonym is a word that means the opposite, or nearly the opposite, of another word. For example, *passive* and *active* are antonyms. Write the Core Word that is an antonym of each word below.

16. meek
17. free

18. perfect
19. constructive

20. offensive

Recall the Words Write the Core Words whose base words are underlined in this recall notice.

1–7.

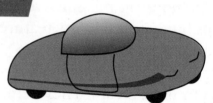

PRODUCT RECALL

Attention Futcherkar owner!

We were recently able to _detect_ that some Futcherkars have faulty brakes. Please _act_ immediately to return your Futcherkar to the nearest dealer. (This notice does _exclude_ model CX550.) Any _defect_ in your brakes will be repaired without charge. We hope that this will not _create_ a problem for you.

We would like to _express_ our apologies for this recall. However, we still believe that no other car can _compare_ to the Futcherkar.

Find the Secret Words An anagram is a word or phrase made by changing the order of letters of another word or phrase. Rearrange the letters in each message and write the Core Word you make. You will need to change the capital letters to lowercase letters.

8. vet to price

9. I move in raft

10. feed vines

11. I travel neat

12. Sarge gives

13. I cured TV set

14. counsel Vic

15. cave pit

Write a letter of complaint about a product. It may be a product you actually own or an imaginary product. Follow the writing process steps on pages 134–135 to write your letter. Use at least four Core Words from this lesson.

Prooofreding a prakticec

1–4. Here is a draft of one student's complaint letter. Find four misspelled Core Words and write them correctly.

> Dear Fleet Sportswear:
>
> Recently, I bought a pair of Fleet Air sneakers. Your ads boast of the shoes' "exclussive, air-filled soles that can take the most agressive use." Well, this must be creative advertising. My shoes fell apart and are clearly deffective. I have no alternitive but to ask for a refund.

Now proofread your own complaint letter and correct any errors.

CORE			CHALLENGE
exclusive	informative	comparative	cooperative
active	captive	defensive	abrasive
protective	aggressive	alternative	cumulative
destructive	detective	conclusive	descriptive
creative	expressive	defective	communicative

32 Spelling Words with *sub-* or *super-*

CORE

1. suburban
2. superhighway
3. subdue
4. superior
5. subsequent
6. superstition
7. submarine
8. supervise
9. substitute
10. superb
11. submerge
12. supermarket
13. substance
14. supersonic
15. subscribe

CHALLENGE

16. supersede
17. subconscious
18. superlative
19. subterranean
20. superintendent

Word Part	Base Word	New Word
sub-	urban	suburban
super-	highway	superhighway

Say each word. Listen to the beginning of each word.

Study the spelling. Can you always find a familiar base word? What meaning does each word part seem to have? Does the meaning change when you add the base word?

Write the words.

1–8. Write the Core Words that begin with *sub-*. Circle any familiar base words.

9–15. Write the Core Words that begin with *super-*. Circle any familiar base words.

16–20. Write the Challenge Words. Circle the *sub-* or *super-* word part.

SPELLING TIP

The word part *sub-* means "under," "down," or "next lower than." The word part *super-* means "over," "above," or "more than." Some words that have the word parts *sub-* or *super-* have familiar base words. Others have spellings that must be remembered.

WORDS and MEANINGS

Write the Core Words that best complete the story.

TALL TALE OR TRUTH?

You really won't believe why it took me so long to buy bread at the (1) last week. Here is the (2) of my story, incredible as it may seem.

Because the (3) was closed to traffic, I had to find a (4) route. This was maddening, since the highway is far (5) to other roads. I drove along the city's outskirts, passing through ordinary (6) neighborhoods. Soon I became lost.

As I was driving around trying to find my way, I found myself thinking about the (7) that bad things happen in threes. Suddenly, my car began to shake. Next, it lifted off the road and took off into the air like a (8) jet! I stepped on the brake to (9) the speed, and at that instant the car dove right into the ocean. I shouted for help, and a (10) surfaced nearby. One of the ship's officers helped to (11) my rescue just as my car began to (12) completely. I received absolutely (13) treatment from the ship's crew, and they even rescued my car a few days later on a (14) mission.

Now, you may (15) to the belief that I made up this story. However, why else would there be seaweed all over the inside of my car?

The Word Part *sub-*
The word part *sub-* can mean "under" or "less than." For example, *submarine* means "under the sea." Add *sub-* to each underlined word or word part and write the word that fits the meaning.

16. underground rail*way*
17. less than *normal*
18. *soil* under surface soil
19. *topic* under another topic
20. *heading* under a main heading

Label the Super Subs
Each submarine can tow three words, but they must be in alphabetical order. Write the Core Word that goes in alphabetical order between the other two words.

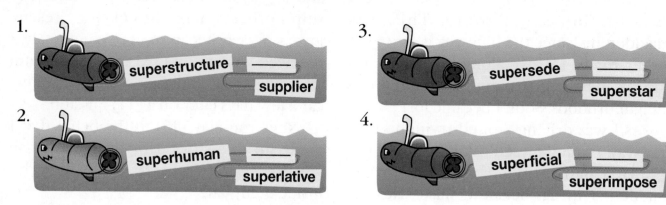

1. superstructure _____ supplier

2. superhuman _____ superlative

3. supersede _____ superstar

4. superficial _____ superimpose

Listen and Write
Write the Core Words that contain the following sounds.

5. the long *e* sound spelled *i-e*
6. the /ü/ sound in its second syllable
7. the /kw/ sound
8. the /j/ sound spelled *g*

Find the Blends
Write the Core Words that contain the underlined consonant combinations.

9. <u>scr</u>ewdriver
10. qui<u>rk</u>
11-12. her<u>b</u>al
13-15. grand<u>st</u>and

Use the Dictionary
Write each word in syllables and then look up its pronunciation in your Speller Dictionary. Circle any letter that spells the /ə/ sound.

16. superstition   17. submarine   18. subscribe   19. suburban   20. superior

Write a tall tale to explain why you were 15 minutes late for school. Follow the writing process steps on pages 134–135 to write your tale. Use at least four Core Words from this lesson.

Proo͡ofreding praktice͡e

1–5. Here is a draft of one student's tall tale. Find five misspelled Core Words and write them correctly.

Dad and I were traveling along the supperhighway when a supersonik spacecraft landed in front of us. It sprayed a green, foamy substanse which began to submerge the car. Then the ship took off. Imagine! This happened right in a suburbun neighborhood! And no, I don't subscreibe to any science fiction magazines.

Now proofread your own tall tale and correct any errors.

CORE			CHALLENGE
suburban	superstition	submerge	supersede
superhighway	submarine	supermarket	subconscious
subdue	supervise	substance	superlative
superior	substitute	supersonic	subterranean
subsequent	superb	subscribe	superintendent

33 Spelling Words with com-, col-, or con-

FOCUS

CORE

1. commission
2. conservation
3. communicate
4. collapse
5. concentrate
6. connect
7. collide
8. committee
9. company
10. college
11. complicate
12. conclusion
13. community
14. collection
15. compound

CHALLENGE

16. compromise
17. conference
18. convey
19. commencement
20. conspiracy

Say each word. Listen for the word part at the beginning of each word.

Study the spelling. How are the word parts spelled? Do you see any base words? Do you see any double consonant spellings?

Write the words.

1–7. Write the Core Words that begin with **com-**. Circle any double consonant spellings.

8–11. Write the Core Words that begin with **col-**. Circle any double consonant spellings.

12–15. Write the Core Words that begin with **con-**. Circle any double consonant spellings.

16–20. Write the Challenge Words. Circle the beginning word part in each word.

SPELLING TIP

The word parts **col-** and **con-** are forms of the word part **com-** that means "with" or "together." **Col-** and **com-** often become part of a double consonant spelling.

A CONSERVATION PLAN

Write the Core Words that best complete the story.

Elena stood nervously before the town council. Her knees began to (1) with one another, and she was afraid she might (2). However, she took a deep breath and spoke.

"The (3) of Bright Falls has a waste problem," she said. "We must (4) on the (5) of trash, which is everywhere. We also need to focus on (6) instead of waste. Why isn't our town recycling? I'd like to form a (7) or a (8) to look into these matters."

The council members began to (9) their thoughts on the subject. Fran Morito, a teacher at the local (10), liked Elena's idea. Ted Lojak, president of a (11) that produced an expensive chemical (12), was not so sure. "I (13) the idea of recycling with higher taxes," he said angrily. The members' discussion grew more heated until Mayor O'Brien stopped them. "Arguing will only (14) our problem," she said. "We need to take a vote and bring this meeting to a (15)."

By a vote of 11 to 1, Elena's plan was approved.

More About *com-*, *col-*, and *con-*

Add *com-*, *col-*, or *con-* to the word parts below to form new words.

16. front
17. position
18. league
19. mend

20. junction
21. bine
22. stellation

Rhyme and Write Write a Core Word to finish the rhyme in each speech balloon.

1. Ours would be a better nation If people practiced ____.

2. If you wish to get more knowledge, You should really go to ____.

3. I read this report with great confusion. The math was bad, is my ____.

4. I have asked the mayor's permission To serve upon the park ____.

Analyze and Write Write Core Words to answer the questions.

5. Which word has three sets of double letters?

6. Which word has the long *i* sound spelled *i-e*?

7–9. Which words have the long *a* sound spelled *a-e*?

10–11. Which words have the long *e* sound spelled *y*?

12. Which word has one pronunciation when it is used as a noun and another pronunciation when it is used as a verb?

13–14. Which words contain the consonant combination *ct*?

15. Which word has the short *a* sound in its second syllable?

Write a list of suggestions for conserving resources and reducing pollution in your area. Use at least four Core Words from this lesson.

Proofreding prakticee

1-4. Here is a draft of one student's list. Find four misspelled Core Words and write them correctly.

1. Build a comunnity recycling center.
2. Try to consentrate on cleaning up public parks.
3. Make every citizen pay extra for excessive waste.
4. Have trash colection twice a week.
5. Form a conservation comission.

Now proofread your own list and correct any errors.

CORE			CHALLENGE
commission	connect	complicate	compromise
conservation	collide	conclusion	conference
communicate	committee	community	convey
collapse	company	collection	commencement
concentrate	college	compound	conspiracy

34 Spelling Words That Describe Excellence

FOCUS

CORE

1. wonderful
2. marvelous
3. astounding
4. supreme
5. fantastic
6. champion
7. brilliant
8. valuable
9. awesome
10. remarkable
11. incredible
12. dazzling
13. admirable
14. ideal
15. outstanding

CHALLENGE

16. miraculous
17. extraordinary
18. magnificent
19. spectacular
20. praiseworthy

Say each word. Listen for familiar vowel and consonant sounds.

Study the spelling. Can you find familiar vowel and consonant spellings? Do you see any familiar suffixes or other word parts?

Write the words.

1–4. Write the Core Words that have two syllables. Underline any familiar suffixes and word parts.

5–11. Write the Core Words that have three syllables. Underline any familiar suffixes and word parts.

12–15. Write the Core Words that have four syllables. Underline any familiar suffixes and word parts.

16–20. Write the Challenge Words. Circle the compound words.

SPELLING TIP

Many words that describe excellence have familiar spellings and word parts.

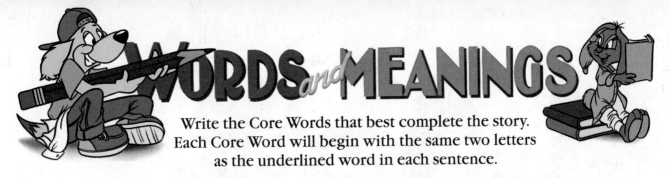

WORDS and MEANINGS

Write the Core Words that best complete the story.
Each Core Word will begin with the same two letters
as the underlined word in each sentence.

SOUTH PACIFIC IS TERRIFIC!

The <u>fabulous</u> Schoolhouse Players put on a (1) performance of *South Pacific* last night. <u>Dashing</u> Tonio Valdez was (2) as the male lead. Arlene Howe, as nurse Nellie Forbush, showed <u>really</u> (3) talent. She <u>wowed</u> everyone with her (4) voice. She <u>brought</u> the audience to its feet with her (5) version of "I'm in Love with a Wonderful Guy."

The supporting cast all <u>added</u> (6) talent. A <u>variety</u> of players made (7) contributions. The <u>inspiring</u> Trini LeVay was (8) in her role as Bloody Mary. Her ability to sing a wide <u>assortment</u> of songs was (9).

The tropical sets <u>made</u> a (10) backdrop for the show. The director had the <u>idea</u> of using real palm trees, which was (11) for creating realism. All of the actors' <u>outfits</u> were (12).

Do not pass up the <u>chance</u> to see this (13) of a musical. You will feel <u>awful</u> if you miss the (14) talents of the cast. In <u>summary</u>, *South Pacific* is simply the Schoolhouse Players' (15) effort.

The Word Part *out-*

The word *outstanding* is made by adding *out-* to the word *standing*. Add *out-* to each word below to write the word that fits each meaning.

come law field going smart

16. the outer part of a baseball diamond
17. to be cleverer than
18. criminal

19. a result
20. friendly and liking to talk

Rewrite the Headlines Each newspaper below has a headline about *South Pacific*. Write a Core Word to replace the newspaper headline.

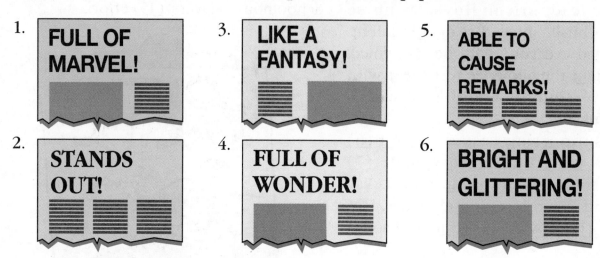

1. **FULL OF MARVEL!**

2. **STANDS OUT!**

3. **LIKE A FANTASY!**

4. **FULL OF WONDER!**

5. **ABLE TO CAUSE REMARKS!**

6. **BRIGHT AND GLITTERING!**

Find the Hidden Word Write the Core Word that rhymes with the underlined word. As you write each word, circle the letters that would fall in the circles below. Then unscramble the circled letters and write the answer to question 11.

7. astonishingly loud <u>pounding</u> — ⊖⊖ — — — — — — ⊖
8. the perfect <u>meal</u> — — ⊖⊖ —
9. an amazing <u>edible</u> — ⊖ — ⊖ — — — — — —
10. a truly ⊖ — — — ⊖ — — football <u>team</u>
11. What is another word for *excellence?*

Listen and Write Write Core Words to answer the questions.

12. Which is the only word that contains the /ô/ sound?
13–17. Which five words have the short *a* sound in the first syllable?

Use the Dictionary Write the entry word that you would look up in a dictionary to find each word below.

18. dazzling   19. craziest   20. comedies

WRITE ON YOUR OWN

Write a review of your favorite book, movie, or TV show. Follow the writing process steps on pages 134–135 to write your review. Use at least four Core Words from this lesson.

Proofreding prakticee

1-5. Here is a draft of a movie review that one student wrote. Find five misspelled Core Words and write them correctly.

> *Checkmate is a really awsome science fiction movie. It is the story of a boy who is a chess champian. To save his planet, he has to win a match against a briliant computer. The plot is outstanding, and the details are fantastick. It keeps you guessing right up to the dazzeling conclusion.*

Now proofread your own review and correct any errors.

CORE			CHALLENGE
wonderful	champion	incredible	miraculous
marvelous	brilliant	dazzling	extraordinary
astounding	valuable	admirable	magnificent
supreme	awesome	ideal	spectacular
fantastic	remarkable	outstanding	praiseworthy

35 Spelling Travel Words

FOCUS

CORE

1. transportation
2. leisure
3. arrangements
4. recreation
5. vacation
6. reservation
7. museum
8. baggage
9. journey
10. cancellation
11. restaurant
12. excursion
13. passenger
14. unusual
15. tourist

CHALLENGE

16. travelogue
17. attendant
18. escape
19. brochure
20. vagabond

Say each word. Listen for familiar vowel and consonant sounds.

Study the spelling. Can you find familiar vowel and consonant spellings? Do you see any familiar prefixes, suffixes, or other word parts? Do you see any surprising or unusual spellings?

Write the words.

1–4. Write the Core Words that have two syllables. Circle any familiar word parts. Underline any unusual spellings.

5–10. Write the Core Words that have three syllables. Circle any familiar word parts. Underline any unusual spellings.

11–15. Write the Core Words that have four syllables. Circle any familiar word parts. Underline any unusual spellings.

16–20. Write the Challenge Words. Circle any consonant blends you find.

SPELLING TIP

Many travel words have familiar spellings and word parts. Some have spellings that must be remembered.

Words and Meanings

Write the Core Words that best complete the story.

Journey to Crete

During your summer __(1)__ from school, how will you spend your __(2)__ time? Would you like to take a __(3)__ to a very __(4)__ place? Then you should travel to Crete, one of the Greek islands.

Crete is a beautiful spot that provides spectacular sights for every visiting __(5)__. Here you can see ancient Greek ruins and artifacts that you would otherwise see only in a __(6)__.

You can make different kinds of __(7)__ for staying on Crete. The fancy hotels are often booked well in advance, but if there is a __(8)__ you may get into one of them on short notice. Or you may make a __(9)__ to stay in a simple lodging house. Each day you can sample wonderful Greek food in a different __(10)__ or take an __(11)__ to a different part of the island. Choose your form of __(12)__—go as a __(13)__ on a tour bus or even on a donkey!

So if your idea of __(14)__ is a new adventure, hurry up and pack your __(15)__ for Crete!

The Suffix -ist

The suffix __-ist__ means "a person who does or makes something." For example, *tourist* means "a person who tours." Write a word with the __-ist__ suffix that means the following.

16. a person who plays the violin
17. a person who writes novels
18. a person who lived in the colonies

19. a person who rides a bicycle or motorcycle
20. a person who drives a motor car

Translate the Greek
Use the key to translate each group of ancient Greek letters below. Write the Core Word you find.

Greek letter	A	E	Γ	I	Λ	M	N	O	Π	P	Σ	T	Y
Modern letter	A	E	G	I	L	M	N	O	P	R	S	T	U

1. PEΣTAYPANT
2. MYΣEYM
3. YNYΣYAΛ
4. TPANΣΠOPTATION
5. APPANΓEMENTΣ
6. TOYPIΣT
7. ΠAΣΣENΓEP
8. ΛEIΣYPE

Take a Close Look
Write the Core Word that matches each clue.

9. It has *a*, *e*, and *g*, but no *r*.
10. It has *u*, *n*, and *o*, but no *y*.
11. It has *v*, *i*, and *a*, but no *c*.
12. It has *i*, *e*, and *l*, but no *u*.

Get to the Core
Write a Core Word to answer each question.

13. Which word has the /ûr/ sound spelled *our?*
14. Which word has the long *a* sound in each of its first two syllables?
15. Which word contains the consonant blend *cr?*

Use the Dictionary
Look up each Core Word below in your Speller Dictionary. Write each word, adding hyphens to show where the word can be broken at the end of a line.

16. leisure
17. restaurant
18. journey
19. transportation
20. excursion

Write a postcard home about a visit to another country.
Use at least four Core Words from this lesson.

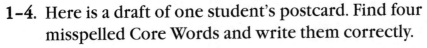

Prooofreding prakticee
(a) (c)

1–4. Here is a draft of one student's postcard. Find four
misspelled Core Words and write them correctly.

Dear Janet,

I am having a great vecation in London England.
Today I went on an excurzion to a wax museum.
Do you know what my transportation was. It was a
double-decker bus! I was hoping the queen would be
a passenjer, but I guess that would be unusual. I
wish you could have joined me on this jurney.

Dick

5–6. This student left out a comma and used an incorrect end
punctuation mark. Copy the postcard and correct the errors.

Now proofread your own postcard and correct any errors.

CORE			CHALLENGE
transportation	reservation	restaurant	travelogue
leisure	museum	excursion	attendant
arrangements	baggage	passenger	escape
recreation	journey	unusual	brochure
vacation	cancellation	tourist	vagabond

Rewrite each phrase or sentence below. Replace the underlined word with a Core Word from Lesson 31. Each word will end with *-ive*. The new phrase or sentence is a famous quotation.

1. "An unhappy <u>choice</u> is before you, Elizabeth."—*Jane Austen*
2. "A sensitive being, a(n) <u>artistic</u> soul."—*William Wordsworth*
3. "Conquering kings their titles take
   From the foes they <u>prisoner</u> make."—*John Chandler*
4. "Man, false man, smiling, <u>harmful</u> man."—*Nathaniel Lee*

Write a Core Word from Lesson 32 that fits each group of words. Each word you write will begin with *sub-* or *super-*.

5. store, grocery, big, ___
6. ship, ocean, underwater, ___
7. after, following, next, ___
8. boss, manage, direct, ___

Write a Core Word from Lesson 33 that is the opposite of each word or phrase below. Each word you will write will begin with *con-*, *com-*, or *col-*.

9. to separate
10. make simple
11. pass by or miss
12. beginning

REVIEW

Write Core Word from Lesson 34 to complete each sentence. Each word is an adjective that begins with the same letter as the underlined word.

13. Molly wrote a ___ <u>book</u> report.
14. We bought ___ <u>fruit</u> at the farmers' market.
15. Oh no, I broke a ___ <u>vase</u>!
16. Jed watched a ___ <u>mystery</u> on TV last night.

Rewrite each sentence. Replace the underlined word or phrase with a Core Word from Lesson 35 that has the same meaning.

17. The taxi driver kindly assisted the lost <u>vacation traveler</u>.
18. Mr. Marquez showed countless blurry slides of his <u>long trip</u> to Nepal.
19. We bravely ordered squid at the <u>eating place</u> in Naples.
20. Our trip to Mexico was too crammed with activities; there was no <u>relaxation</u> time.

Steps in the Writing Process

Here are some steps you might want to use to help you write.

1 **Prewriting**

Think about what you want to write about.
What have you done or seen?
What things do you remember?
Ask a friend for ideas.

Explore your topic.
Make a list of things that pop into your head.
Draw a picture or diagram of your idea.
Share your thoughts with others.

2 **Drafting**

Make a first try at writing your paper.
Write quickly to get your ideas down.
Do not worry about mistakes now.

3 Revising

Carefully read what you have written.

Change your words, sentences, or ideas to make them better.

Read your writing to someone else. Ask him or her how
to make it better.

4 Proofreading

Read what you have written again.

Look for errors in spelling, capitalization, and punctuation,
and correct them.

5 Publishing

Make a clean, neat copy of what you have written.

Be careful not to make new mistakes.

Add pictures, a title, or other special things.

Share your writing with others.

How to Use the Dictionary

The word you look up in a dictionary is called an **entry word.** A dictionary tells you how to spell and pronounce the word. It also gives one or more definitions for the word.

The entry words in a dictionary are arranged in alphabetical order. If two words have the same first letter, they are put in alphabetical order using the second letter.

Study the dictionary entries below. Notice how much you can learn about a word from a dictionary.

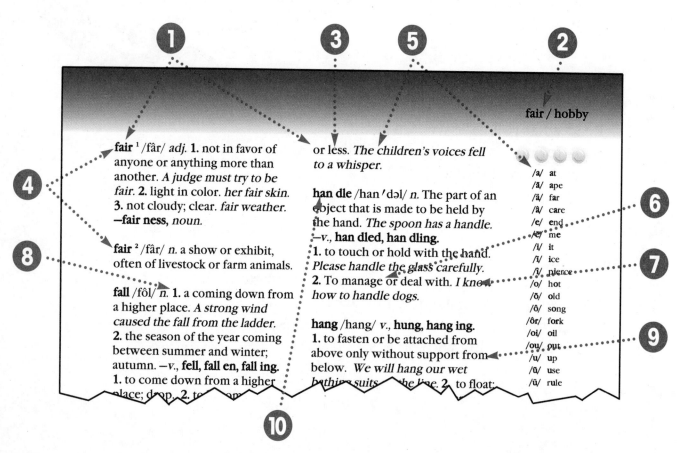

1 **3** **5** **2**

fair / hobby

4

fair [1] /fâr/ *adj.* **1.** not in favor of anyone or anything more than another. *A judge must try to be fair.* **2.** light in color. *her fair skin.* **3.** not cloudy; clear. *fair weather.* **—fair ness,** *noun.*

8

fair [2] /fâr/ *n.* a show or exhibit, often of livestock or farm animals.

fall /fôl/ *n.* **1.** a coming down from a higher place. *A strong wind caused the fall from the ladder.* **2.** the season of the year coming between summer and winter; autumn. —*v.,* **fell, fall en, fall ing. 1.** to come down from a higher place; drop. **2.** to ____

or less. *The children's voices fell to a whisper.*

han dle /han′dəl/ *n.* The part of an object that is made to be held by the hand. *The spoon has a handle.* —*v.,* **han dled, han dling. 1.** to touch or hold with the hand. *Please handle the glass carefully.* **2.** To manage or deal with. *I know how to handle dogs.*

hang /hang/ *v.,* **hung, hang ing. 1.** to fasten or be attached from above only without support from below. *We will hang our wet bathing suits on the line.* **2.** to float;

/a/	at
/ā/	ape
/ä/	far
/â/	care
/e/	end
/ē/	me
/i/	it
/ī/	ice
/î/	pierce
/o/	hot
/ō/	old
/ô/	song
/ôr/	fork
/oi/	oil
/ou/	out
/u/	up
/ū/	use
/ü/	rule

6

7

9

10

1 The **entry word** is the word you look up. Entry words are in bold type and listed in alphabetical order.

2 At the top of each dictionary page are two words called **guide words.** They are the first and last entry words appearing on that page. Guide words help you find an entry word quickly.

3 Words with more than one syllable are shown in two parts. A space separates the syllables.

4 Sometimes there is more than one entry for a word. When this happens, each entry is numbered.

5 After the entry word is the **pronunciation.** It is given between two lines. Special letters are used to show how to pronounce the the word. A **pronunciation key** shows the sound for each special letter. The pronunciation key is found on each page of the dictionary.

6 An abbreviation for the **part of speech** of the entry word is given after the pronunciation.

7 The dictionary also shows **irregular forms** of the entry word. If an **-s, -es, -ed,** or **-ing** is simply added to the word, the dictionary does not list these regularly spelled forms.

8 One or more **definitions** are given for each entry word. If there is more than one definition, the definitions are numbered.

9 Sometimes the entry word is used in a **sample sentence** or phrase to help explain the meaning of the entry word.

10 Some words can be more than one part of speech. If so, the dictionary sometimes gives another definition for the entry word.

Speller Dictionary

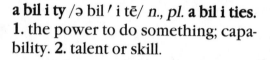

a bil i ty /ə bil ′ i tē/ *n.,* *pl.* **a bil i ties.**
1. the power to do something; capability. **2.** talent or skill.

-able a suffix used to form adjectives that means **1.** able to be. **2.** worthy of being.

a bol ish /ə bol ′ ish/ *v.* to end; stop.

a bra sive /ə brā ′ siv, ə brā ′ ziv/ *n.* a substance used for cleaning, grinding, or polishing. —*adj.* harsh or irritating in manner. *an abrasive person.* —**a bra sive ly,** *adv.,* —**a bra sive ness,** *n.*

ab sent /ab sənt/ *adj.* **1.** not present; away. **2.** not existing; missing. *Leaves are absent on trees in winter.*

ab sorp tion /ab sôrp ′ shən, ab zôrp ′ shən/ *n.* **1.** the act or process of absorbing. **2.** complete attention; engrossment.

a bun dance /ə bun ′ dəns/ *n.* a very large amount; a quantity that is more than enough.

ac cent /ak ′ sent, ak sent ′/ *n.* **1.** the stress or stronger tone of voice given to a word or part of a word. *In the word "happy," the accent is on the first syllable.* **2.** a mark used on a word to show which syllable is spoken with an accent. **3.** a particular way in which people from a certain part of a country or from a foreign country pronounce words. —*v.* to pronounce or mark a word or syllable with a stronger tone of voice.

ac cent mark /ak ′ sent märk/ *n.* a mark used on a word to show which syllable is spoken with an accent or stronger tone of voice.

ac ci dent /ak ′ si dənt/ *n.* **1.** something that happens for no apparent reason and is unexpected. **2.** an unfortunate event that is not expected.

ac ci den tal ly /ak ′ si den ′ tə lē, ak ′ sə dent ′ lē/ *adv.* by chance.

ac com plish ment
/ə kom ′ plish mənt/ *n.* **1.** the act of accomplishing; completion. **2.** something accomplished; achievement. **3.** a special skill or ability that is usually gained by training.

138

ac cu rate /ak ′ yər it/ *adj.* **1.** being correct, exact, or precise. **2.** making few or no errors or mistakes; exact. **—ac cu rate ly,** *adv.* **—ac cu rate ness,** *n.*

a chieve ment /ə chēv ′ mənt/ *n.* something accomplished or achieved.

ac quaint ance /ə kwān ′ təns/ *n.* **1.** a person one knows, but who is not a close friend. **2.** knowledge of something gained from experience.

ac tive /ak ′ tiv/ *adj.* moving around or doing something much of the time; lively; busy. **—ac tive ly,** *adv.* **—ac tive ness,** *n.*

ac tiv i ty /ak tiv ′ i tē/ *n., pl.* **ac tiv i ties. 1.** the condition of doing something or moving around; action; movement. **2.** a thing to do or to be done.

ad di tion /ə dish ′ ən/ *n.* **1.** the adding of two or more numbers. **2.** the act of adding. **3.** something that is added. *to build an addition to the house.*

ad jec tive /aj ′ ik tiv/ *n.* a word that describes or modifies a noun or pronoun. In the sentence "The large suitcase is green," the words "large" and "green" are adjectives.

ad mi ra ble /ad ′ mər ə bəl/ *adj.* worthy of approval or respect. **—ad mi ra ble ness,** *n.* **—ad mi ra bly,** *adv.*

ad mi ral /ad ′ mər əl/ *n.* a naval officer of the highest rank.

ad mis sion /ad mish ′ ən/ *n.* **1.** the act of allowing to enter. **2.** the price a person must pay to enter. **3.** the act of making known that something is true; confession.

ad ven tur ous /ad ven ′ chər əs/ *adj.* **1.** willing to risk danger in order to have exciting or unusual experiences; bold. **2.** full of danger or risk. **—ad ven tur ous ly,** *adv.* **—ad ven tur ous ness,** *n.*

ad verb /ad ′ vûrb/ *n.* a word that describes or modifies a verb, an adjective, or another adverb. In the sentence "Two very large vans drove quite slowly down the street," the words "very," "quite," and "slowly" are adverbs.

ad vice /ad vīs ′/ *n.* an idea that is offered to a person about how to solve a problem or how to act in a certain situation; suggestion; recommendation.

ag gres sive /ə gres ′ iv/ *adj.* **1.** ready and eager to attack or start a fight. **2.** very forceful and bold. **—ag gres sive ly,** *adv.* **—ag gres sive ness,** *n.*

a gree ment /ə grē ′ mənt/ *n.* **1.** an understanding between people or groups. **2.** the condition of agreeing; harmony.

al ge bra /al ′ jə brə/ *n.* the branch of mathematics that deals with the relations between known and unknown numbers. In an algebra problem letters are used to stand for unknown numbers. In the algebra problem $X + Y = 7$, if $X = 3$, then $Y = 4$.

/a/	at
/ā/	ape
/ä/	far
/â/	care
/e/	end
/ē/	me
/i/	it
/ī/	ice
/î/	pierce
/o/	hot
/ō/	old
/ô/	song
/ôr/	fork
/oi/	oil
/ou/	out
/u/	up
/ū/	use
/ü/	rule
/u/	pull
/ûr/	turn
/ch/	chin
/ng/	sing
/sh/	shop
/th/	thin
/th/	this
/hw/	white
/zh/	treasure
/ə/	about
	taken
	pencil
	lemon

al ley /al ′ ē/ *n.* a narrow street or passageway between or behind buildings.

al li ga tor /al ′ i gā tər/ *n.* an animal with a long head and tail and a thick, tough skin. Alligators live in rivers and swamps in the southeastern United States and China. Alligators are reptiles. They are closely related to crocodiles but have shorter, wider heads.

al low ance /ə lou ′ əns/ *n.* **1.** a sum of money or quantity of something given at regular times or set aside for a particular purpose. **2.** discount or reduction. **3.** the act of allowing or conceding; acceptance. *the court's allowance of a claim.*

adj. adjective
adv. adverb
conj. conjunction
contr. contraction
def. definition
interj. interjection
n. noun
pl. plural
prep. preposition
pron. pronoun
sing. singular
v. verb
v.i. intransitive verb
v.t. transitive verb

al ma nac /ôl ′ mə nak ′/ *n.* **1.** a book that contains facts and figures on many different subjects. Almanacs are published every year. **2.** a book that gives facts about the weather, the tides, and the rising and setting of the sun for each day of the year.

al pha bet /al ′ fə bet ′/ *n.* the letters or characters that are used to write a language, arranged in their proper order.

al ter nate /ôl ′ tər nāt ′, ôl ′ tər nit/ *v.* **al ter nat ed, al ter nat ing. 1.** to take turns. **2.** to happen or appear with one thing following another. —*adj.* **1.** happening or appearing one after another. **2.** first one, then the other.—*n.* a person or thing that takes the place of another; substitute. —**al ter nate ly,** *adv.* —**al ter na tion,** *n.*

al ter na tive /ôl tûr ′ nə tiv/ *n.* **1.** a choice between two or more things. *We had the alternative of going to the beach or on a picnic.* **2.** one of two or more things that may be chosen.

am bi tious /am bish ′ əs/ *adj.* **1.** having a strong desire to succeed at something; having ambition. **2.** requiring great ability or effort. *an ambitious plan.* —**am bi tious ly,** *adv.* —**am bi tious ness,** *n.*

a muse ment /ə mūz ′ mənt/ *n.* **1.** the condition of being amused and entertained. **2.** something that amuses or entertains.

an noy ance /ə noi ′ əns/ *n.* **1.** a person or thing that annoys. **2.** the condition of being annoyed.

an nu al /an ′ ū əl/ *adj.* **1.** measured by the year. **2.** happening or returning once a year. *an annual holiday.* —*n.* a plant that lives only one year or growing season. —**an nu al ly,** *adv.*

an ten na /an ten ′ ə/ *n., pl.* **an ten nas** *(def. 1)* or **an ten nae** /an ten ′ ē/ *(def. 2)* **1.** a metallic device, such as a rod or wire, used to send out or receive radio or television signals. **2.** one of a pair of long, thin body parts, such as that on the head of an insect or a lobster; feelers. Antennae are used to sense touch and smells.

ap par ent /ə par ′ ənt/ *adj.* **1.** easily seen or understood. **2.** seeming real or true even though it may not be. *The apparent size of a star is much smaller than its real size.* —**ap par ent ly,** *adv.*

ap pear ance /ə pir ′ əns/ *n.* **1.** the act of appearing or coming into sight. **2.** the way a person or thing looks; outward look. **3.** the act of coming before the public.

ap plaud /ə plôd ′/ *v.* **1.** to show approval or enjoyment of something by clapping the hands. **2.** to approve or praise.

a quar i um /ə kwâr ′ ē əm/ *n., pl.* **a quar i ums** or **a quar i a**/ə kwâr ′ ē ə/ **1.** a tank, bowl, or similar container in which fish, other water animals, and water plants are kept. **2.** a building used to display collections of fish, other water animals, and water plants.

ar e a /âr ′ ē ə/ *n.* **1.** the amount of surface within a given boundary. **2.** a particular space; region, or section.

Ar gen ti na /är ′ jən tē ′ nə/ *n.* a country in southern South America.

ar range ment /ə rānj ′ mənt/ *n.* **1.** the act of putting in order or position. **2.** something arranged. **3. ar range ments.** plans or preparations. *We made arrangements for our class party.*

ar ti cle /är ′ ti kəl/ *n.* **1.** a composition written for a newspaper, magazine, or book. **2.** a particular thing or object, item. **3.** any one of the words *a, an,* or *the* used to modify a noun.

art ist /är ′ tist/ *n.* **1.** a person who is skilled in painting, music, literature, or any other form of art. **2.** a person whose work shows talent or skill.

as sist ant /ə sis ′ tənt/ *n.* a person who assists; helper; aide. —*adj.* acting to assist another person. *the head coach and four assistant coaches.*

as sort ment /ə sôrt ′ mənt/ *n.* a collection of different kinds. *a large assortment of sports equipment.*

as ter oid /as ′ tə roid′/ *n.* any of the thousands of small planets that revolve around the sun. Most of them are between the orbits of Mars and Jupiter.

as ton ish /ə ston ′ ish/ *v.* to surprise very much; amaze.

as ton ish ment /ə ston ′ ish mənt/ *n.* great surprise; amazement.

as tound /ə stound ′/ *v.* to surprise very much; amaze; astonish. —**as tound ing ly,** *adv.*

as tro naut /as ′ trə nôt ′/ *n.* a person trained to fly in a spacecraft.

as tron o mer /ə stron ′ ə mər/ *n.* a person who works or specializes in astronomy, a science that deals with the sun, moon, stars, planets, and other heavenly bodies.

-ate a suffix used to form adjectives from nouns or to form verbs. When used to form adjectives it means relating to or having; when used to form verbs it means to become or cause to become.

/a/	at
/ā/	ape
/ä/	far
/â/	care
/e/	end
/ē/	me
/i/	it
/ī/	ice
/î/	pierce
/o/	hot
/ō/	old
/ô/	song
/ôr/	fork
/oi/	oil
/ou/	out
/u/	up
/ū/	use
/ü/	rule
/ù/	pull
/ûr/	turn
/ch/	chin
/ng/	sing
/sh/	shop
/th/	thin
/th/	this
/hw/	white
/zh/	treasure
/ə/	about
	taken
	pencil
	lemon

ath le tic /ath let ′ ik/ *adj.* **1.** of or having to do with an athlete or athletics. **2.** active and strong. —**ath let i cal ly,** *adv.*

at mos phere /at ′ məs fîr ′/ *n.* **1.** the layer of gases that surround the Earth. The atmosphere is made up of oxygen, nitrogen, carbon dioxide, and other gases. **2.** the air in a particular place. **3.** character or mood.

at ten dant /ə ten ′ dənt/ *n.* a person who takes care of someone or provides service to other people.

au di to ri um /ô ′ di tôr ′ ē əm/ *n.* a large room or building where a group of people can gather.

adj.	adjective
adv.	adverb
conj.	conjunction
contr.	contraction
def.	definition
interj.	interjection
n.	noun
pl.	plural
prep.	preposition
pron.	pronoun
sing.	singular
v.	verb
v.i.	intransitive verb
v.t.	transitive verb

au thor /ô ′ thər/ *n.* a person who has written a book, story, play, article, or other work of literature.

awe some /ô ′ səm/ *adj.* causing wonder or fear. *The huge whale was an awesome sight.* —**awe some ly,** *adv.* —**awe some ness,** *n.*

aw ful /ô ′ fəl/ *adj.* **1.** causing fear, dread, or awe; terrible. **2.** very bad. **3.** very large; great.

awk ward /ôk ′ wərd/ *adj.* **1.** lacking grace or poise in movement or behavior; clumsy or uncomfortable. **2.** difficult or embarrassing. **3.** difficult to use or handle. —**awk ward ly,** *adv.* —**awk ward ness,** *n.*

aw ning /ô ′ ning/ *n.* a cover of canvas, metal, or other material that serves as a small roof over a door or window. An awning is used as a shelter.

bag gage /bag ′ ij/ *n.* the suitcases, trunks, or bags that a person takes when going on a trip.

barge /bärj/ *n.* a boat with a flat bottom. —*v.* **barged, barg ing. 1.** to move clumsily and abruptly. **2.** to enter rudely or heedlessly. *to barge into a meeting.*

bar ri er /bar ′ ē ər/ *n.* something that blocks the way.

Bel gium /bel ′ jəm/ *n.* a country in northwestern Europe.

be tray /bi trā ′/ *v.* **1.** to give help to the enemy of. **2.** to be unfaithful to. —**be tray al,** *n.* —**be tray er,** *n.*

bi- a prefix that means having or involving two.

bi an nu al /bī an ′ ū əl/ *adj.* happening twice a year; semiannual. —**bi an nu al ly,** *adv.*

bi cen ten ni al /bī ′ sen ten ′ ē əl/ *adj.* happening once every 200 years. —*n.* a 200th anniversary or its celebration.

bi ceps /bī ′ seps/ *n., pl.* **bi ceps** or **bi ceps es.** the large muscle that runs down the front of the arm from the shoulder to the elbow. When it is contracted, the arm bends.

bi cy cle /bī si kəl/ *n.* a light vehicle with two wheels, one behind the other. It has a seat, handlebars to steer with, and two foot pedals to turn the wheels and make it go forward.

bi noc u lars /bə nok ′ yə lərs, bī nok ′ yə lərs/ *n.* a device that makes distant objects look larger and closer. Binoculars are made up of two small telescopes joined together, so that a person can look at distant objects with both eyes.

bois ter ous /boi ′ stər əs/ *adj.* noisy and lively. *a boisterous party.*
—bois ter ous ly, *adv.*
—bois ter ous ness, *n.*

Bot swa na /bot swä ′ nə/ *n.* a country in south-central Africa.

bou quet /bō kā ′, bü kā ′/ *n.* a bunch of flowers.

Bra zil /brə zil ′/ *n.* a country in eastern South America.

breathe /brē<u>th</u>/ *v.,* **breathed, breath ing.** to draw air into the lungs and then release it.

breath less /breth ′ lis/ *adj.* **1.** out of breath. **2.** holding the breath because of excitement or fear. *The children were breathless as they watched the acrobats at the circus.* **—breath less ly,** *adj.* **—breath less ness,** *n.*

bril liant /bril ′ yənt/ *adj.* **1.** very bright; sparkling. **2.** very fine; splendid. **3.** very intelligent. **—bril liant ly,** *adv.*

broc co li /brok ′ ə lē/ *n.* a plant whose thick green stems and flower buds are eaten as a vegetable.

bro chure /brō shùr ′/ *n.* a small pamphlet; booklet. *an advertising brochure.*

bul le tin /bùl ′ i tin/ *n.* **1.** a short announcement of the latest news. **2.** a small newspaper or magazine published regularly.

bur den /bûr ′ dən/ *n.* **1.** something that is carried; load. **2.** something very hard to bear. *—v.* to put too heavy a load on. *Snow burdened the branches.*

bur glar /bûr ′ glər/ *n.* a person who breaks into a house, store, or other place to steal something.

busi ness /biz ′ nis/ *n., pl.* **busi ness es. 1.** the work that a person does to earn a living. **2.** an activity that is carried on to make money, along with the place and equipment used. **3.** the buying and selling of things; trade. **4.** matters or affairs. **—busi ness like,** *adj.*

· · · C · · · · · · · · · · · · · · · · · ·

ca boose /kə büs ′/ *n.* a railroad car that is at the end of a freight train. The train crew live, rest, or work in the caboose.

cac tus /kak ′ təs/ *n., pl.* **cac ti, cac tus es, cac tus.** a plant that has a thick stem covered with spines instead of leaves.

/a/	at
/ā/	ape
/ä/	far
/â/	care
/e/	end
/ē/	me
/i/	it
/ī/	ice
/î/	pierce
/o/	hot
/ō/	old
/ô/	song
/ôr/	fork
/oi/	oil
/ou/	out
/u/	up
/ū/	use
/ü/	rule
/ù/	pull
/ûr/	turn
/ch/	chin
/ng/	sing
/sh/	shop
/th/	thin
/<u>th</u>/	this
/hw/	white
/zh/	treasure
/ə/	about
	taken
	pencil
	lemon

143

cal cu late /kal ′ kyə lāt ′/ *v.* **cal cu lat ed, cal cu lat ing. 1.** to find out by using addition, subtraction, multiplication, or division. **2.** to estimate by examining numbers or quantities.

cal cu la tor /kal ′ kyə lā tər/ *n.* a small computer that can solve mathematical problems. Many calculators run on batteries and can be held in one hand.

cal en dar /kal ′ ən dər/ *n.* **1.** a chart showing the days, weeks, and months of a year. **2.** a schedule of events that will take place.

adj. adjective
adv. adverb
conj. conjunction
contr. contraction
def. definition
interj. interjection
n. noun
pl. plural
prep. preposition
pron. pronoun
sing. singular
v. verb
v.i. intransitive verb
v.t. transitive verb

cam er a /kam ′ ər ə, kam ′ rə/ *n.* a device for taking photographs or motion pictures. A camera consists of a box with a small hole. When the hole is uncovered, light enters the camera and makes an image on the film inside. Most cameras have a lens to focus the image on the film.

Can a da /kan ′ ə də/ *n.* a country in North America that is north of the United States.

can cel /kan ′ səl/ *v.* **1.** to decide not to do, have, or go; call off. **2.** to cross out or mark with a line or lines to show that it cannot be used again.

can cel la tion /kan ′ sə lā ′ shən/ *n.* **1.** the act of canceling or state of being canceled. **2.** something that is canceled.

cap tive /kap ′ tiv/ *n.* a person or animal that is captured and held by force; prisoner. *—adj.* held prisoner. *The captive lion was kept in a cage.*

cap ture /kap ′ chər/ *v.* **cap tured, cap tur ing. 1.** to catch and hold a person, animal, or thing. **2.** to attract and hold. *The film captured my interest.* *—n.* the act of catching and holding a person, animal, or thing.

car bon /kär ′ bən/ *n.* a chemical element that is found in all living things and in coal and charcoal. Diamonds and graphite are carbon in the form of crystals.

car toon /kär tün ′/ *n.* a drawing, often with words or a caption, that shows people or things in a way that makes you laugh.

catch /kach/ *v.* **1.** to take or get hold of something or someone that is moving. **2.** to come upon suddenly; surprise. **3.** to get; receive. *to catch a cold.*

caught /kôt/ *v.* past tense and past participle of *catch.*

cause /kôz/ *n.* **1.** a person or thing that makes something happen. **2.** something a person or group believes in. *—v.,* **caused, caus ing.** to make something happen; result in.

cau tious /kô ′ shəs/ *adj.* using caution; careful. *Always be cautious when you ride your bicycle.* **—cau tious ly,** *adv.* **—cau tious ness,** *n.*

ceil ing /sē ′ ling/ *n.* the inside overhead surface of a room.

cel e brate /sel ′ ə brāt ′/ *v.* **cel e brat ed, cel e brat ing.** to observe or honor a special day or event with ceremonies and other activities.

cem e ter y /sem ′ i ter ′ ē/ *n., pl.* **cem e ter ies.** a place where the dead are buried.

cen sus /sen ′ səs/ *n., pl.* **cen sus es.** an official count of the people living in a country or district. A census is taken to find out how many people there are, and their age, sex, and kind of work.

cen ter /sen ′ tər/ *n.* **1.** the middle point of a circle or sphere. **2.** the middle point, part, or place of something. —*v.* to put in or at the center.

cen ti me ter /sen ′ tə mē ′ tər/ *n.* a unit of length in the metric system. A centimeter is equal to 1/100 of a meter. One inch equals about two and a half centimeters.

cen tu ry /sen ′ chə rē/ *n., pl.* **cen tu ries.** a period of one hundred years. From 1651 to 1750 is one century.

ce ra mic /sə ram ′ ik/ *adj.* made of baked clay. —*n.* an object made of baked clay.

cer tain /sûr ′ tən/ *adj.* **1.** sure; positive. **2.** known but not named; some; particular. *Certain animals hunt for food at night.*

cer tif i cate /sər tif ′ i kit/ *n.* a written statement that is accepted as proof of certain facts.

cham ber /chām ′ bər/ *n.* **1.** a room in a house or other building. **2.** the office of a judge, usually in a courthouse. **3.** a hall where a lawmaking body meets.

cham pi on /cham ′ pē ən/ *n.* **1.** a person or thing that is the winner of first place in a contest or game. **2.** a person who fights or speaks for another person or a cause. *The senator is a champion of the rights of the poor.*

chan nel /chan ′ əl/ *n.* **1.** the deepest part of a river, harbor, or other waterway. **2.** a band of frequencies that a radio or television station uses to send out electronic signals.

cha os /kā ′ os/ *n.* complete confusion; great disorder. *The village was in chaos after the earthquake.*

char ac ter /kar ′ ik tər/ *n.* **1.** all the qualities that make a person or thing different from others. **2.** strength of mind, courage, and honesty taken together. **3.** a person in a book, play, story, or motion picture. **4.** a person who is different, funny, or strange.

char coal /chär ′ kōl/ *n.* a soft, black substance that is a form of carbon. It is made by partially burning wood or other plant or animal matter. Charcoal is used as a fuel and in pencils for drawing.

ched dar /ched ′ ər/ *n.* any of several types of hard, smooth cheese, ranging in color from white to orange and in taste from strong and sharp to mild.

chem is try /kem ′ ə strē/ *n., pl.* **chem is tries.** the science that deals with substances, what they are made of, what characteristics they have, and what kinds of changes happen when they combine with other substances.

/a/	at
/ā/	ape
/ä/	far
/â/	care
/e/	end
/ē/	me
/i/	it
/ī/	ice
/î/	pierce
/o/	hot
/ō/	old
/ô/	song
/ôr/	fork
/oi/	oil
/ou/	out
/u/	up
/ū/	use
/ü/	rule
/ů/	pull
/ûr/	turn
/ch/	chin
/ng/	sing
/sh/	shop
/th/	thin
/th/	this
/hw/	white
/zh/	treasure
/ə/	about
	taken
	pencil
lemon	

chief tain /chēf ′ tən/ *n.* a leader of a tribe or clan.

child /chīld/ *n., pl.* **chil dren.** a young boy or girl.

chim ney /chim ′ nē/ *n.* an upright, hollow structure that is connected to a fireplace or furnace. It carries away the smoke from the fire.

chlo rine /klôr ′ ēn/ *n.* a greenish-yellow, poisonous gas that has a strong, unpleasant odor. Chlorine is used to kill germs and to bleach things. Chlorine is a chemical element.

adj.   adjective
adv.   adverb
conj.   conjunction
contr.   contraction
def.   definition
interj.   interjection
n.   noun
pl.   plural
prep.   preposition
pron.   pronoun
sing.   singular
v.   verb
v.i.   intransitive verb
v.t.   transitive verb

choc o late /chô ′ kə lit, chok ′ ə lit/ *n.* a food substance made from cacao beans that have been roasted and ground. Chocolate is used to make drinks and candy.

choice /chois/ *n.* **1.** the act or result of choosing. **2.** the chance to choose. **3.** a person or thing that is chosen. —*adj.* **choic er, choic est.** of very good quality; excellent.

cho rus /kôr ′ əs/ *n., pl.* **cho rus es. 1.** a group of people who sing or dance together. **2.** a part of a song that is sung after each stanza. —*v.* **cho rused, cho rus ing.** to sing or say at the same time.

chrome /krōm/ *n.* another word for chromium, a hard, brittle, silver-white metallic element. It is used to plate metals and in alloys to provide strength and resistance to corrosion.

chro mo some /krō ′ mə sōm ′/ *n.* a tiny structure in the nuclei of living cells, composed chiefly of proteins and DNA. Chromosomes carry the genes that determine sex, size, color, and many other characteristics.

chron o log i cal /kron ′ ə loj ′ i kəl/ *adj.* arranged according to the order in which events happened. —**chron o log i cal ly,** *adv.*

chry san the mum /krə san ′ thə məm/ *n.* a round flower with many small petals. Chrysanthemums may be yellow, white, or some other color.

chuck le /chuk ′ əl/ *v.* **chuck led, chuck ling.** to laugh in a quiet way. When we chuckle we are often laughing to ourselves.

churn /chûrn/ *n.* a container in which cream or milk is shaken or beaten to make butter. —*v.* **1.** to shake or beat cream or milk in a special container to make butter. **2.** to stir or move with a forceful motion.

cir cle /sûr ′ kəl/ *n.* a closed curved line made up of points that are all the same distance from a point inside called the center. —*v.* **cir cled, cir cling. 1.** to make a circle around. **2.** to move around in a circle.

cir cuit /sûr ′ kit/ *n.* **1.** a movement around. **2.** the path of an electric current. Electricity in a house moves in a circuit that takes it from wires outside the house to the different wall sockets, switches, and appliances in the house.

cir cu lar /sûr ′ kyə lər/ *adj.* having or making the shape of a circle; round. —*n.* a letter or advertisement that is sent to many people. —**cir cu lar ly,** *adv.*

cir cum fer ence /sər kum ′ fər əns/ *n.*
1. a curved line that forms the outside edge of a circle. **2.** the distance
around something.

cir cum stance /sûr ′ kəm stans ′/ *n.* a
condition, act, or event that exists or
happens along with other things and
that may have an effect on them.
*Weather is a circumstance beyond
our control.*

ci ta tion /sī tā ′ shən/ *n.* **1.** the act of
citing or quoting. **2.** the passage or
words quoted; quotation. **3.** a public
commendation or award for bravery
or outstanding achievement. **4.** a
summons to appear before a court
of law.

cit rus /sit ′ rəs/ *adj.* of or having to
do with a group of trees whose fruits
are juicy and often have a thick rind.

civ il /siv ′ əl/ *adj.* **1.** having to do
with a citizen or citizens. **2.** polite but
not friendly; courteous. *I was very
angry but still managed to give a civil
answer.*

clean li ness /klen ′ lē nis/ *n.* the condition of being clean; the habit of
always keeping clean.

clev er /klev ′ ər/ *adj.* **1.** having a
quick mind; bright and alert. **2.** showing skill or intelligence. —**clev er ly,**
adv. —**clev er ness,** *n.*

col- a form of the prefix *com-* before *l.*

col lapse /kə laps ′/ *v.* **col lapsed,**
col laps ing. 1. to fall in; break down
or fail. *The explosion caused the
walls of the house to collapse.* **2.** to

lose strength or health. —*n.* the act of
falling in, breaking down, or failing.

col lec tion /kə lek ′ shən/ *n.* **1.** a gath-
ering together. **2.** a group of things
gathered together. *a collection of
dinosaur bones.* **3.** money that is
collected.

col lege /kol ′ ij/ *n.* a school that
offers more advanced education than
high school. A college gives degrees
to show that a person has completed
certain studies.

col lide /kə līd ′/ *v.* **col lid ed,**
col lid ing. 1. to crash against each
other. **2.** to disagree very strongly;
clash. *The mayor collided with the
governor over plans for a new highway.*

col li sion /kə lizh ′ ən/ *n.* the act of
colliding; a crash.

colo nel /kûr ′ nəl/ *n.* an officer in the
armed forces. In the United States
Army, Marine Corps, or Air Force, a
colonel ranks below a general but
above a major.

col umn /kol ′ əm/ *n.* **1.** an upright
structure shaped like a post; pillar.
2. a narrow, vertical section of printed words on a page. **3.** a part of a
newspaper written regularly by one
person. **4.** a long row or line.

com- a prefix that means in associa-
tion with; together.

com bine /kəm bīn ′/ *v.* **com bined,**
com bin ing. to join together; unite.
/kom ′ bīn/—*n.* a farm machine that
harvests and threshes grain.

/a/	at
/ā/	ape
/ä/	far
/â/	care
/e/	end
/ē/	me
/i/	it
/ī/	ice
/î/	pierce
/o/	hot
/ō/	old
/ô/	song
/ôr/	fork
/oi/	oil
/ou/	out
/u/	up
/ū/	use
/ü/	rule
/u̇/	pull
/ûr/	turn
/ch/	chin
/ng/	sing
/sh/	shop
/th/	thin
/th/	this
/hw/	white
/zh/	treasure
/ə/	about
	taken
	pencil
lemon	

com et /kom ′ it/ *n.* a bright object in space that looks like a star with a long tail of light. A comet is made up of ice, frozen gases, and dust particles. A comet travels along an oval path around the sun.

com ma /kom ′ ə/ *n.* a punctuation mark (,) that is used to separate words, phrases, or clauses in a sentence.

com mence ment /kə mens ′ mənt/ *n.* 1. a beginning; a start. *January 1 marks the commencement of a new year.* 2. the day or ceremony of graduation.

com mer cial /kə mûr ′ shəl/ *adj.* relating to business or trade. —*n.* an advertising message on radio or television. —**com mer cial ly,** *adv.*

com mis sion /kə mish ′ ən/ *n.* 1. a group of persons who are chosen to do certain work. 2. money for work done. 3. the act of committing. 4. a position of military rank. 5. a thing that a person or persons is asked and trusted to do.

com mit tee /kə mit ′ ē/ *n.* a group of persons who are chosen to do certain work.

com mu ni cate /kə mū ′ ni kāt ′/ *v.* **com mu ni cat ed, com mu ni cat ing.** to exchange or pass along feelings, thoughts, or information.

com mu ni ca tive /kə mū ′ ni kā ′ tiv, kə mū ′ ni kə tiv/ *adj.* ready to communicate or disclose information,

talkative. —**com mu ni ca tive ly,** *adv.* —**com mu ni ca tive ness,** *n.*

com mu ni ty /kə mū ′ ni tē/ *n., pl.* **com mu ni ties.** 1. a group of people who live together in the same place. 2. a group of people who share a common interest.

com mu ter /kə mū ′ tər/ *n.* a person who travels a long distance to and from work and school.

com pa ny /kum ′ pə nē/ *n., pl.* **com pa nies.** 1. a guest or guests. 2. a business firm or organization. 3. companionship.

com par a tive /kəm par ′ ə tiv/ *adj.* having to do with or showing a comparison of one thing with another. —*n.* the form of an adjective or adverb that shows a greater degree or more of whatever is expressed by the basic form. For example, "taller" is the comparative of "tall." —**com par a tive ly,** *adv.*

com pare /kəm pâr ′/ *v.* **com pared, com par ing.** 1. to study in order to find out how persons or things are alike or different. 2. to say or think that something is like something else.

com pli ance /kəm plī ′ əns/ *n.* 1. the act of agreeing or giving in. *In compliance with the doctors orders, I stayed home until my cold was better.* 2. readiness or tendency to give in to others.

com pli cate /kom ′ pli kāt ′/ *v.* **com pli cat ed, com pli cat ing.** to make hard to understand or do. *My friends' attempts to help only complicated the job of washing the car.*

com pound /kom ′ pound, kəm pound′/ *adj.* made up of two or more parts. —*v.* to mix or combine. —*n.* **1.** a mixture or combination. **2.** a word that is made up of two or more words. The words *comic strip, merry-go-round,* and *nighttime* are compounds.
—**com pound a ble,** *adj.*
—**com pound er,** *n.*

com pro mise /kom ′ prə mīz ′/ *n.* the settlement of an argument or dispute by agreeing that each side will give up parts of its demands. —*v.* **com pro mised, com pro mis ing.** to reach a settlement by agreeing that each side will give up some part of its demands. *When the two children wanted to watch different television programs, they compromised and watched parts of both.*

con- the form of the prefix **com-** before all consonants except *b, h, l, m, p, r,* and *w.*

con cen trate /kon ′ sən trāt ′/ *v.* **con cen trat ed, con cen trat ing. 1.** to bring together into one place. **2.** to make stronger or thicker. **3.** to pay close attention. —**con cen tra tor,** *n.*

con ces sion /kən sesh ′ ən/ *n.* **1.** the act of conceding or yielding. *My parents made a concession and let me stay up late.* **2.** something that is conceded.

con clu sion /kən klü ′ zhən/ *n.* **1.** the end of something. **2.** arrangement; settlement. **3.** something decided after thinking.

con clu sive /kən klü ′ siv/ *adj.* ending argument or doubt; final. *The arrow-* heads were conclusive evidence that Indians once lived in the area.
—**con clu sive ly,** *adv.*
— **con clu sive ness,** *n.*

con di tion /kən dish ′ ən/ *n.* **1.** the way that a person or thing is; the state something is in. **2.** something needed for another event or thing to occur; something required. **3.** an illness or an unhealthy state of the body or a part of the body. —*v.* **1.** to put in a healthy state or good shape. **2.** to make used to something. *to become conditioned to the heat.*

con fer ence /kon ′ fər əns/ *n.* a meeting to talk over important matters.

con fi dent /kon ′ fi dənt/ *adj.* **1.** having trust or faith; sure. *I am confident that our team will win.* **2.** having faith in oneself or one's own abilities.

con gress /kong ′ gris/ *n., pl.* **con gress es. 1.** an assembly of people who make laws. **2. Congress.** a branch of the government of the United States that makes laws. Congress is made up of the Senate and the House of Representatives.

con junc tion /kən jungk ′ shən/ *n.* **1.** a word that joins other words or groups of words. In the sentence "My friends and I were late because we missed the bus," the words "and" and "because" are conjunctions. **2.** the act of joining together or the state of being joined together.

con nect /kə nekt ′/ *v.* **1.** to fasten or join together. **2.** to consider as related; associate. *We connect robins with spring.* —**con nect er;** *also,* **con nec tor,** *n.*
—**con nect i ble,** *adj.*

/a/ at
/ā/ ape
/ä/ far
/â/ care
/e/ end
/ē/ me
/i/ it
/ī/ ice
/î/ pierce
/o/ hot
/ō/ old
/ô/ song
/ôr/ fork
/oi/ oil
/ou/ out
/u/ up
/ū/ use
/ü/ rule
/ù/ pull
/ûr/ turn
/ch/ chin
/ng/ sing
/sh/ shop
/th/ thin
/th/ this
/hw/ white
/zh/ treasure
/ə/ about
taken
pencil
lemon

con se quence /kon ′ si kwens ′/ *n.*
1. the result of an action. *One conse-quence of going to sleep late at night is waking up tired.* **2.** significance; importance.

con ser va tion /kon ′ sər vā ′ shən/ *n.*
1. the act of conserving. **2.** the protection and wise use of the forests, rivers, minerals, and other natural resources of a country.

con so nant /kon ′ sə nənt/ *n.* a letter of the alphabet that is not a vowel. Consonants include the letters *b, d, f, g, m, p, t,* and others.

con spir a cy /kən spir ′ ə sē/ *n., pl.*
con spir a cies. secret planning together with others to do something wrong. *Some members of a gang were arrested for conspiracy to rob a bank.*

con stel la tion /kon ′ stə lā ′ shən/ *n.* a group of stars. A constellation forms a pattern in the sky that looks like a picture. *The Big Dipper and the Little Dipper are parts of constellations.*

con sume /kən süm ′/ *v.* **con sumed, con sum ing. 1.** to use up or destroy. **2.** to eat or drink up. **—con sum a ble,** *adj.*

con tin u ous /kən tin ′ ū əs/ *adj.* going on without stopping; unbroken. **—con tin u ous ly,** *adv.* **—con tin u ous ness,** *n.*

con trac tion /kən trak ′ shən/ *n.*
1. the act of contracting or the state of being contracted. *The contraction of the heart forces blood into the arteries.* **2.** a shortened form. *Wouldn't is a contraction of would not.*

con ven ience /kən vēn ′ yəns/ *n.*
1. ease and comfort. *I like the conve-nience of canned foods.* **2.** something that gives ease or comfort.

con vey /kən vā ′/ *v.* **1.** to take from one place to another; carry. **2.** to make known; express. *My parents conveyed the excitement of their trip in their letters.*

co op er a tion /kō op ′ ə rā ′ shən/ *n.* the act of working together.

co op er a tive /kō op ′ ər ə tiv, kō op ′ ə rā ′ tiv/ *adj.* willing to work together with another or others. *a very cooperative coworker.* **—n.** a business enterprise, such as a food store or farm produce distributor, that is owned and operated by its members, who share its profits.
—co op er a tive ly, *adv.*
—co op er a tive ness, *n.*

cor dial /kôr ′ jəl/ *adj.* warm and friendly; hearty. *The mayor gave us a cordial greeting when we arrived.*
—cor dial ly, *adv.*

cor ri dor /kôr ′ i dər, kor ′ i dər/ *n.* a long hallway or passageway in a building. A corridor often has rooms opening onto it.

cough /kôf/ *v.* **1.** to force air from the lungs with a sudden, sharp sound. **2.** to make a noise like coughing. **—n.** the sound that is made when air is suddenly forced from the lungs.

count /kount/ *v.* **1.** to find out how many of something there are; add up. **2.** to say or write down numbers in order. **3.** to include or be included when things are added up. **4.** to have importance; to be worth something. **5.** to depend; rely. —*n.* the number of things there are when you add them up; total.

coun try /kun ′ trē/ *n., pl.* **coun tries.** **1.** any area of land; region. **2.** an area of land that has boundaries and has a government that is shared by all the people; nation. *The United States is a country.* **3.** the people of a country. —*adj.* having to do with land outside of cities or towns; rural.

cour te ous /kûr ′ tē əs/ *adj.* having good manners; polite.
—**cour te ous ly,** *adv.*
—**cour te ous ness,** *n.*

cre a tive /krē ā ′ tiv/ *adj.* having or showing ability to make or do something in a new way. *A creative person did this unusual painting.*
—**cre a tive ly,** *adv.* —**cre a tive ness,** *n.*

crev ice /krev ′ is/ *n.* a narrow crack into or through something. *The wind blew in through the crevices in the walls of the cabin.*

cru el ty /krü ′ əl tē/ *n., pl.* **cru el ties.** **1.** the causing of pain or suffering to others. **2.** a cruel act.

cruise /krüz/ *v.* **cruised, cruis ing.** **1.** to sail from place to place. **2.** to move or ride from place to place. —*n.* a boat trip taken for pleasure.

cru sade /krü sād ′/ *n.* **1.** any of the military expeditions undertaken by the Christian people of Europe between the years 1095 and 1291 to take Palestine away from the Muslims. **2.** a strong fight against something evil or for something good. —*v.* **cru sad ed, cru sad ing.** to fight in a crusade.

cru sad er /krü sād ′ ər/ *n.* a person who fights in a crusade.

cu mu la tive /kü ′ myə lə tiv/ *adj.* increasing in size, strength, or value by constant additions. *The cumulative evidence from experiments finally led to acceptance of the theory.*
—**cu mu la tive ly,** *adv.*
—**cu mu la tive ness,** *n.*

cyl in der /sil ′ ən dər/ *n.* **1.** a solid or hollow object that is shaped like a drum or a soup can. **2.** a chamber in which the piston of an engine or pump moves.

• • • **D** • • • • • • • • • • • • • •

dan ger /dān ′ jər/ *n.* **1.** the chance that something bad or harmful will happen. **2.** something that may cause harm or injury.

dan ger ous /dān ′ jər əs/ *adj.* likely to cause something bad or harmful to happen. *Driving too fast is dangerous.* —**dan ger ous ly,** *adv.*
—**dan ger ous ness,** *n.*

/a/	at
/ā/	ape
/ä/	far
/â/	care
/e/	end
/ē/	me
/i/	it
/ī/	ice
/î/	pierce
/o/	hot
/ō/	old
/ô/	song
/ôr/	fork
/oi/	oil
/ou/	out
/u/	up
/ū/	use
/ü/	rule
/ù/	pull
/ûr/	turn
/ch/	chin
/ng/	sing
/sh/	shop
/th/	thin
/th/	this
/hw/	white
/zh/	treasure
/ə/	about
	taken
	pencil
	lemon

daugh ter /dô ′ tər/ *n.* a female child.

daz zle /daz ′ əl/ *v.* **daz zled, daz zling. 1.** to make almost blind by too much light. **2.** to impress with something very showy or brilliant. —**daz zler,** *n.* —**daz zling ly,** *adv.*

de ci sion /di sizh′ ən/ *n.* the act or result of making up one's mind.

de fec tive /di fek ′ tiv/ *adj.* having a flaw or weakness; not perfect. *Defective electrical wiring is a cause of fires in homes.* —**de fec tive ly,** *adv.* —**de fec tive ness,** *n.*

de fen sive /di fen ′ siv/ *adj.* guarding or protecting against attack. *Knights used to put on defensive armor before going into battle.* —**de fen sive ly,** *adv.* —**de fen sive ness,** *n.*

de fi ance /di fī ′ əns/ *n.* bold refusal to obey or respect authority.

def i ni tion /def ′ ə nish ′ ən/ *n.* an explanation of the meaning of a word or group of words.

de nom i na tor /di nom ′ ə nā ′ tər/ *n.* the number below the line in a fraction. The denominator shows the number of equal parts into which the whole is divided. In the fraction 1/2, 2 is the denominator.

de par ture /di pär ′ chər/ *n.* the act of departing or going away. *The plane's departure was delayed two hours.*

de pen dence /di pen ′ dəns/ *n.* the state of relying on someone else for what is needed or wanted.

de pres sion /di presh ′ ən/ *n.* **1.** sadness; gloom. **2.** a low place or hollow. *The car bumped over a depression in the road.* **3.** a time when business is slow and people are out of work.

de scrip tive /di skrip ′ tiv/ *adj.* giving a picture in words. *The tourists were given descriptive pamphlets about places to visit.* —**de scrip tive ly,** *adv.* —**de scrip tive ness,** *n.*

des ert [1] /dez ′ ərt/ *n.* a hot, dry, sandy area of land with few or no plants growing on it. —*adj.* not lived in or on; desolate. *The sailor was shipwrecked on a desert island.*

de sert [2] /di zûrt ′/ *v.* to go away and leave a person or thing that should not be left; abandon. *The soldiers deserted their company.* —**de sert er,** *n.*

des per ate /des ′ pər it/ *adj.* **1.** reckless because of having no hope. A desperate person is ready or willing to try anything. *The desperate player hurled the basketball at the net just as the game was ending.* **2.** very bad or hopeless. *a desperate situation.* —**des per ate ly,** *adv.* —**des per ate ness,** *n.*

des sert /di zûrt ′/ *n.* a food served at the end of a meal. Fruit, pie, cheese, and ice cream are desserts.

de struc tive /di struk ′ tiv/ *adj.* causing destruction. *Moths can be destructive to clothes made of wool.* —**de struc tive ly,** *adv.* —**de struc tive ness,** *n.*

adj. adjective
adv. adverb
conj. conjunction
contr. contraction
def. definition
interj. interjection
n. noun
pl. plural
prep. preposition
pron. pronoun
sing. singular
v. verb
v.i. intransitive verb
v.t. transitive verb

de tec tive /di tek ′ tiv/ *n.* a police officer or other person whose work is finding information about crimes and trying to solve them. —*adj.* having to do with detectives and their work. *Do you like to read detective stories?*

de vel op ment /di vel ′ əp mənt/ *n.* 1. the act or process of developing. *The development of a spacecraft that could reach the moon took many years.* 2. an event or happening. —**de vel op men tal**, *adj.*

de vote /di vōt ′/ *v.* **de vot ed, de vot ing.** to give effort, attention, or time to some purpose; dedicate.

dif fer ence /dif ′ ər əns, dif ′ rəns/ *n.* 1. the state or quality of being unlike or different. 2. the amount left after one quantity is subtracted from another; remainder. *The difference between 16 and 12 is 4.*

dif fer ent /dif ′ ər ənt, dif ′ rənt/ *adj.* 1. not alike or similar. 2. not the same; separate. *It rained two different times this afternoon.*

di ges tion /di jes ′ chən, dī jes ′ chən/ *n.* the process of breaking down food into a form that can be absorbed and used by the body. Digestion starts in the mouth and is completed in the intestines.

dis as trous /di zas ′ trəs/ *adj.* causing or accompanied by disaster. *a disastrous flood.* —**dis as trous ly**, *adv.*

dis card /dis kärd ′, dis ′ kärd/ *v.* to throw aside or give up as useless, worthless, or not wanted.

dis ci pline /dis ′ ə plin/ *n.* 1. training that develops skill, good character, orderly behavior. 2. punishment given to train or correct someone. —*v.* **dis ci plined, dis ci plin ing.** 1. to train to be obedient. 2. to punish.

dis con nect /dis ′ kə nəkt ′/ *v.* to separate from another part or from a source of electricity; break the connection of. —**dis con nec tion**, *n.*

dis count /dis ′ kount ′/ *n.* an amount subtracted from the regular price. *I bought a suit on sale at 25 percent discount.*

dis cuss /di skus ′/ *v.* to talk over; speak about. *My friends and I discussed our plans.*

dis cus sion /di skush ′ ən/ *n.* the act of talking something over; a serious exchange of opinions.

dis loy al /dis loi ′ əl/ *adj.* going against one's allegiance; not loyal; unfaithful. —**dis loy al ly**, *adj.*

dis miss /dis mis ′/ *v.* 1. to send away or allow to leave. 2. to take away the job of; fire.

dis po si tion /dis ′ pə zish ′ ən/ *n.* 1. a person's usual way of acting, thinking, or feeling; nature. *You always have a cheerful disposition.* 2. a natural tendency.

dis solve /di zolv ′/ *v.* **dis solved, dis solv ing.** 1. to mix thoroughly and evenly with a liquid. *Dissolve the powder in milk to make the instant pudding.* 2. to bring to an end. —**dis solv a ble**, *adj.*

/a/	at
/ā/	ape
/ä/	far
/â/	care
/e/	end
/ē/	me
/i/	it
/ī/	ice
/î/	pierce
/o/	hot
/ō/	old
/ô/	song
/ôr/	fork
/oi/	oil
/ou/	out
/u/	up
/ū/	use
/ü/	rule
/u̇/	pull
/ûr/	turn
/ch/	chin
/ng/	sing
/sh/	shop
/th/	thin
/th/	this
/hw/	white
/zh/	treasure
/ə/	about
	taken
	pencil
	lemon

153

dis tance /dis ′ təns/ *n.* **1.** the amount of space between two things or points. **2.** a point or place that is far away.

dis trust /dis trust ′/ *v.* to have no trust or confidence in; be suspicious of; doubt. —*n.* lack of trust or confidence; suspicion.

dis turb ance /di stûr ′ bəns/ *n.* **1.** an interruption. **2.** something that disturbs. *The laughter was a disturbance to the students who were reading.*

div i dend /div ′ i dend/ *n.* **1.** a number that is to be divided by another number. *When you divide 6 by 3 the dividend is 6.* **2.** money that is earned by a business; profit.

di vi sion /di vish′ ən/ *n.* **1.** the act of dividing or the condition of being divided. *The division of the house into apartments provided homes for five families.* **2.** one of the parts into which something is divided. **3.** something that divides or separates.

drow sy /drou ′ zē/ *adj.* **drow si er, drow si est.** half asleep; sleepy. *I felt drowsy after dinner and decided to take a nap.* —**drow si ly,** *adv.* —**drow si ness,** *n.*

du pli cate /dü ′ pli kit, dū ′ pli kit, dü ′ pli kāt ′, dū pli kāt ′/ *adj.* just like something else. —*n.* something that is just like something else; exact copy. —*v.* **du pli cat ed, du pli cat ing. 1.** to make an exact copy of something. **2.** to do again; repeat.

· · · **E** · · · · · · · · · · ·

Earth /ûrth ′/ *n.* the planet on which we live. It is the fifth largest planet in our solar system and the third planet in order of distance from the sun.

ech o /ek ′ ō/ *n., pl.* **ech oes.** the repeating of a sound. Echoes are caused when sound waves bounce off a surface. —*v.* **1.** to send back the sound of something. **2.** to be heard again. **3.** to repeat or imitate closely.

e clipse /i klips ′/ *n.* a darkening or hiding of the sun, a planet, or a moon by another heavenly body. In an eclipse of the sun, the moon passes between the sun and the earth. In an eclipse of the moon, the earth moves between the sun and the moon. —*v.* **e clipsed, e clips ing. 1.** to cause an eclipse of. **2.** to be better or more important than.

e con o my /i kon′ ə mē/ *n., pl.* **e con o mies. 1.** the way a country produces, distributes, and uses its money, goods, natural resources, and services. **2.** the careful use of money and other things to reduce waste.

Ec ua dor /ek ′ wə dôr ′/ *n.* a country in northwestern South America. —**Ec ua do ri an,** *adj., n.*

e di tion /i dish ′ ən/ *n.* **1.** the form in which a book is printed. **2.** the total number of copies of a book, newspaper, or magazine printed at one time. **3.** one of the copies of a book, newspaper, or magazine printed at one time.

E gypt /ē ′ jipt/ *n.* a country in the Middle East. Ancient Egypt was the center of one of the world's earliest civilizations.

em bar rass /em bar ′ əs/ *v.* to make someone feel shy, uncomfortable, or ashamed.

em per or /em ′ pər ər/ *n.* the ruler of an empire.

-ence a suffix used in nouns that means the action, quality, state, or condition of being.

en chant ment /en chant ′ mənt/ *n.* the act of enchanting or being enchanted. *The enchantment of the kingdom by the magical spell was to last one hundred years.*

en cour age ment /en kûr ij mənt, en kur ′ ij mənt/ *n.* **1.** the act of encouraging or the condition of being encouraged. **2.** something that encourages or gives courage, hope, or confidence.

en dur ance /en dùr ′ əns, en dyùr ′ əns/ *n.* the power to put up with hardships or difficulties. *The pioneers who crossed the wilderness in covered wagons had much endurance.*

Eng lish /ing ′ glish/ *n.* **1.** a language spoken in England, the United States, Canada, India, Australia, and many other places. **2. the English.** the people of England. —*adj.* **1.** of England or its people. **2.** of or in the English language.

-ent a suffix used to form adjectives that means being or acting in a particular state or manner.

e qual i ty /i kwol ′ i tē/ *n.* the quality or condition of being equal or the same. *The Constitution of the United States provides for the equality of all Americans under the law.*

e qua tor /i kwā ′ tər/ *n.* an imaginary line around the earth. It is halfway between the North and South Poles. The United States and Canada are north of the equator. Most of South America is south of the equator.

e quip ment /i kwip ′ mənt/ *n.* anything that is provided for a particular purpose or use; supplies.

-er a suffix that means more.

e rase /i rās ′/ *v.*, **e rased, e ras ing.** **1.** to remove by rubbing, scratching, or wiping off. **2.** to remove recording from. *I accidentally erased a part of the tape.*

es cape /e skāp ′/ *v.* **es caped, es cap ing. 1.** to get free. **2.** to remain free from. —*n.* **1.** the act of escaping. **2.** a way of escaping.

es say /es ′ ā/ *n.* a short written composition on a subject.

-est a suffix that means most.

es tab lish /e stab ′ lish/ *v.* **1.** to begin or create; set up. *The college established a new course for students.* **2.** to show or prove to be true.

e ter ni ty /i tûr ′ ni tē/ *n., pl.* **e ter ni ties. 1.** time without beginning or end; all time. **2.** a period of time that seems endless.

/a/	at
/ā/	ape
/ä/	far
/â/	care
/e/	end
/ē/	me
/i/	it
/ī/	ice
/î/	pierce
/o/	hot
/ō/	old
/ô/	song
/ôr/	fork
/oi/	oil
/ou/	out
/u/	up
/ū/	use
/ü/	rule
/ù/	pull
/ûr/	turn
/ch/	chin
/ng/	sing
/sh/	shop
/th/	thin
/th/	this
/hw/	white
/zh/	treasure
/ə/	about
	taken
	pencil

lemon

adj. adjective
adv. adverb
conj. conjunction
contr. contraction
def. definition
interj. interjection
n. noun
pl. plural
prep. preposition
pron. pronoun
sing. singular
v. verb
v.i. intransitive verb
v.t. transitive verb

ev i dent /ev ′ i dənt/ *adj.* easily seen or understood; clear.

ex ag ger ate /eg zaj ′ ə rāt ′/ *v.* **ex ag ger at ed, ex ag ger at ing.** to make something seem larger, greater, or more important than it is.

ex clu sive /ek sklü ′ siv/ *adj.* **1.** belonging to a single person or group. **2.** open to a certain kind of person or group only. **3.** complete; entire. *The students gave the visitor their exclusive attention.*
—**ex clu sive ly,** *adv.*
—**ex clu sive ness,** *n.*

ex cur sion /ek skûr ′ zhən, ek skûr ′ shən/ *n.* **1.** a short trip made for a special reason or for pleasure. *The class took an excursion to the zoo.* **2.** a trip, as on an airplane or train, at a reduced fare.

ex pe ri ence /ek spir ′ ē əns/ *n.* **1.** something that a person has done, seen, or taken part in. **2.** the knowledge or skill a person gains from doing something. —*v.* **ex pe ri enced, ex pe ri enc ing.** to have something happen to one; feel; undergo.

ex plo sion /ek splō ′ zhən/ *n.* **1.** the act of bursting or expanding suddenly and noisily. **2.** a sudden outburst. *The funny joke caused an explosion of laughter.*

ex pres sive /ek spres ′ iv/ *adj.* full of meaning or feeling. *The poet read the poem in a very expressive voice.*
—**ex pres sive ly,** *adv.*
—**ex pres sive ness,** *n.*

ex ten sion /ek sten ′ shən/ *n.* **1.** the act of extending or the condition of being extended. **2.** something that extends; addition. **3.** an extra telephone added to the same line as the main telephone.

ex traor di nar y /ek strôr ′ də ner ′ē, ek strə ôr ′ də ner ′ ē/ *adj.* very unusual; remarkable.
—**ex traor di nar i ly,** *adv.*

● ● ●**F**● ● ● ● ● ● ● ● ● ● ● ● ● ● ● ● ● ●

fa mil iar /fə mil ′ yər/ *adj.* **1.** often heard or seen. **2.** known because of having been heard or seen before. **3.** knowing something well.
—**fa mil iar ly,** *adv.*

fa mous /fā ′ məs/ *adj.* very well-known; having great fame.

fan tas tic /fan tas ′ tik/ *adj.* **1.** very strange; odd. **2.** very good; excellent.
—**fan tas ti cal ly,** *adv.*

fau cet /fô ′ sit/ *n.* a device for turning on or off the flow of water or another liquid from a pipe, sink, or container.

fault y /fôl ′ tē/ *adj.* **fault i er, fault i est.** having faults or defects. *faulty reasoning.* —**fault i ly,** *adv.*
—**fault i ness,** *n.*

fierce /fîrs/ *adj.* **fierc er, fierc est.**
1. likely to make violent attacks; dangerous; savage. **2.** very strong or violent; raging. *The fierce storm blew down several trees.* —**fierce ly,** *adv.*
—**fierce ness,** *n.*

fier y /fīr ′ ē, fī ′ ə rē/ *adj.* **fier i er,**
fier i est. 1. made up of fire. *a fiery*
furnace. **2.** hot as fire; burning. *the*
fiery sands of the desert. **3.** full of
feeling. *a fiery speech.* **4.** excitable.
a fiery temper. —**fier i ly,** *adv.*
—**fier i ness,** *n.*

fool ish /fü ′ lish/ *adj.* without good
sense; unwise. —**fool ish ly,** *adv.*
—**fool ish ness,** *n.*

foot /fut/ *n., pl.* **feet. 1.** the end part
of the leg that humans and other animals walk on or stand on. **2.** a measure of length equal to twelve inches.

for mal i ty /fôr mal ′ i tē/ *n., pl.*
for mal i ties. 1. proper or very polite
behavior. **2.** a correct or official procedure. **3.** something that is a matter
of form only.

for ma tion /fôr mā ′ shən/ *n.* **1.** the
process of forming or making.
2. something formed or made.
unusual rock formations. **3.** the way
in which the members or units of a
group are arranged.

for mu la /fôr ′ myə lə/ *n., pl.*
for mu las or **for mu lae** /fôr ′ myə lē ′/.
1. an explanation of how to prepare a
medicine, food, or other mixture. **2.** a
rule expressed in symbols or numbers. **3.** a set method for doing or getting something.

for tress /fôr ′ tris/ *n., pl.* **for tress es.**
a strong place that can be defended
against attack; fort.

for tu nate /fôr ′ chə nit/ *adj.* having
or resulting from good luck; lucky.
—**for tu nate ly,** *adv.*

frac tion /frak ′ shən/ *n.* **1.** a part of a
whole. **2.** a number that stands for
one or more of the equal parts of a
whole. A fraction shows the division
of one number by a second number.
2/3, 3/4, and 1/16 are fractions.

fraud /frôd/ *n.* **1.** a tricking of someone in order to cheat. **2.** a person or
thing that tricks or cheats; fake.

fur ther /fûr ′ thər/ *adj.* **1.** a comparative of *far.* **2.** additional; more. *with-*
out further delay. —*adv.* **1.** at or to a
more distant point in time or space;
farther. **2.** to a greater degree or
extent; more. *to inquire further into*
a problem. —*v.* to help forward;
support.

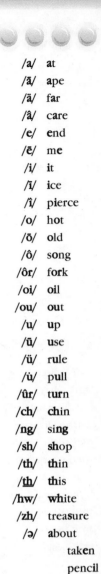

··· **G** ·········· **G** ···

gal lon /gal ′ ən/ *n.* a unit of measure
for liquids. A gallon equals four
quarts or about 3.8 liters.

gauge /gāj/ *n.* **1.** a standard of measurement. **2.** an instrument for measuring. —*v.* **gauged, gaug ing. 1.** to
measure. **2.** to estimate. —**gauge a ble,**
adj. **gaug er,** *n.*

ge og ra phy /jē og ′ rə fē/ *n., pl.*
ge og ra phies. 1. the science that
deals with the surface of the earth
and the plant, animal, and human
life on it. When you study geogra-
phy, you learn about the earth's
countries and people, and about
its climate, oceans and rivers,
mountains, and natural resources. **2.**
the surface or natural features of a
place or region.

/a/	at
/ā/	ape
/ä/	far
/â/	care
/e/	end
/ē/	me
/i/	it
/ī/	ice
/î/	pierce
/o/	hot
/ō/	old
/ô/	song
/ôr/	fork
/oi/	oil
/ou/	out
/u/	up
/ū/	use
/ü/	rule
/u̇/	pull
/ûr/	turn
/ch/	chin
/ng/	sing
/sh/	shop
/th/	thin
/th/	this
/hw/	white
/zh/	treasure
/ə/	about
	taken
	pencil

lemon

ge om e try /jē om ′ i trē/ *n., pl.*
ge om e tries. a branch of mathematics that deals with the measurement and relation of points, lines, angles, plane figures, and solids.

Ger ma ny /jûr mə nē/ *n.* a country in north central Europe.

gnash /nash/ *v.* to strike, grate, or grind (the teeth) together, as in anger or pain.

gnaw /nô/ *v.* to bite again and again in order to wear away little by little. *The dog gnawed the bone.*

adj. adjective
adv. adverb
conj. conjunction
contr. contraction
def. definition
interj. interjection
n. noun
pl. plural
prep. preposition
pron. pronoun
sing. singular
v. verb
v.i. intransitive verb
v.t. transitive verb

go ril la /gə ril ′ ə/ *n.* a large, very strong animal that is a kind of ape. Gorillas have big, heavy bodies, short legs, and long arms. They live in Africa.

grav i ty /grav ′ i tē/ *n., pl.* **grav i ties.** the force that pulls things toward the center of the earth. **2.** serious nature. *Because of the gravity of the situation, troops were sent in.*

graze [1] /grāz/ *v.* to feed on growing grass.

graze [2] /grāz/ *v.* to scrape or touch lightly in passing.

great /grāt/ *adj.* **1.** very large in size, number, or amount. **2.** very important, excellent, or remarkable. **3.** more than usual; much. —**great ness,** *n.*

Great Bri tain /grāt brit ′ ən/ *n.* an island off the western coast of Europe. Great Britain includes the countries of England, Scotland, and Wales.

group /grüp/ *n.* a number of persons or things together. —*v.* to form or put into a group or groups.

guar an tee /gar ′ ən tē ′/ *n.* **1.** a promise to repair or replace something or to give back the money for it, if anything goes wrong with it before a certain time has passed. **2.** anything that makes an outcome or condition certain. —*v.* **guar an teed, guar an tee ing. 1.** to give a guarantee for. **2.** to promise something.

guard i an /gär ′ dē ən/ *n.* **1.** a person or thing that guards or watches over. **2.** a person chosen by law to take care of someone who is young or who is not able to care for himself or herself.

guest /gest/ *n.* **1.** a person who is at another's house for a meal or visit. **2.** a customer in a restaurant, hotel, or similar place.

guid ance /gī ′ dəns/ *n.* **1.** the act or process of showing how or directing; direction. **2.** advice concerning one's plans for attending school or getting a job.

guilt /gilt/ *n.* **1.** the condition or fact of having done something wrong or having broken the law. **2.** a feeling of having done something wrong; shame.

guilt y /gil ′ tē/ *adj.* **guilt i er, guilt i est. 1.** having done something wrong or having committed a crime; deserving to be blamed or punished. **2.** feeling or showing guilt or shame. —**guilt i ly,** *adv.*

gui tar /gi tär´/ *n.* a musical instrument with a long neck and six or more strings. It is played by plucking or strumming the strings.

ham mock /ham´ ək/ *n.* a swinging bed that is hung between two trees or poles. It is made from a long piece of canvas or netting.

hap py /hap´ ē/ *adj.* **hap pi er, hap pi est. 1.** feeling or showing pleasure or gladness. **2.** satisfied and pleased with one's condition; contented.

har ness /här´ nis/ *n., pl.* **har ness es.** the straps, bands, and other gear used to attach a work animal to a cart, plow, or wagon. —*v.* **1.** to put a harness on. **2.** to control and make use of. *At that dam, engineers harness water power to generate electricity.*

hast y /hās´ tē/ *adj.* **hast i er, hast i est. 1.** quick; hurried. **2.** too quick; careless or reckless. —**hast i ly,** *adv.* —**hast i ness,** *n.*

haugh ty /hô´ tē/ *adj.* **haugh ti er, haugh ti est.** thinking of oneself as much better than other people; arrogant. *a haughty king.* —**haugh ti ly,** *adv.* —**haugh ti ness,** *n.*

haunch /hônch/ *n., pl.* **haunch es.** a part of the body of a person or animal including the hip and upper thigh.

haunt /hônt/ *v.* **1.** to visit or live in. *Some people say that ghosts haunt the old house.* **2.** to come often to the mind of.

head ache /hed´ āk / *n.* **1.** a pain felt inside the head. **2.** something that causes trouble or worry.

herb /ûrb, hûrb/ *n.* a plant whose leaves, stems, seeds, or roots are used in cooking for flavoring, in medicines, or because they are fragrant. *Mint and parsley are herbs.*

his tor ic /hi stôr´ ik/ *adj.* important in history.

hon es ty /on´ ə stē/ *n.* the quality of being honest; truthfulness.

hos til i ty /ho stil´ i tē/ *n., pl.* **hos til i ties.** a readiness to fight; unfriendliness; antagonism. *There was still hostility between the two old enemies.*

hu man i ty /hū man´ i tē, ū man´ i tē/ *n., pl.* **hu man i ties. 1.** people; all human beings. **2.** deep concern for the suffering of others; human sympathy.

hu mid i ty /hū mid´ i tē, ū mid´ i tē/ *n.* water vapor in the air; dampness. *The high humidity made us feel warm and uncomfortable.*

hu mor ous /hū´ mər əs, ū´ mər əs/ *adj.* making people laugh; funny; comical. —**hu mor ous ly,** *adv.* —**hu mor ous ness,** *n.*

hur ri cane /hûr´ i kān, hur´ i kān´/ *n.* a storm with very strong winds and heavy rain.

/a/	at
/ā/	ape
/ä/	far
/â/	care
/e/	end
/ē/	me
/i/	it
/ī/	ice
/î/	pierce
/o/	hot
/ō/	old
/ô/	song
/ôr/	fork
/oi/	oil
/ou/	out
/u/	up
/ū/	use
/ü/	rule
/u̇/	pull
/ûr/	turn
/ch/	chin
/ng/	sing
/sh/	shop
/th/	thin
/th/	this
/hw/	white
/zh/	treasure
/ə/	about
	taken
	pencil
	lemon

hus tle /hus ′ əl/ *v.* **hus tled, hus tling.** to move or do something very quickly and with energy.

hy phen /hī ′ fən/ *n.* a punctuation mark (-) that is used to connect two or more words or parts of words to form a compound word, as in the word *merry-go-round.* A hyphen is also used to connect the syllables of a word that has been divided at the end of a line.

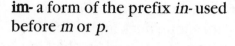

adj. adjective
adv. adverb
conj. conjunction
contr. contraction
def. definition
interj. interjection
n. noun
pl. plural
prep. preposition
pron. pronoun
sing. singular
v. verb
v.i. intransitive verb
v.t. transitive verb

-ic a suffix used to form adjectives from nouns that means having to do with; being or like.

i de al /ī dē ′ əl/ *n.* a person or thing thought of as perfect. —*adj.* being exactly what one would hope for; perfect.

il le gal /i lē ′ gəl/ *adj.* not legal; against laws or rules. —**il le gal ly,** *adv.*

il leg i ble /i lej ′ ə bəl/ *adj.* very hard or impossible to read. —**il leg i bil i ty,** *n.* —**il leg i bly,** *adv.*

il lit er ate /i lit ′ ər it/ *adj.* not able to read or write. —**il lit er ate ly,** *adv.*

il log i cal /i loj ′ i kəl/ *adj.* **1.** not logical. **2.** showing a lack of good sense or reasoning. —**il log i cal ly,** *adv.*

il lu mi nate /i lü ′ mə nāt ′/ *v.* **il lu mi nat ed, il lu mi nat ing.** To light up; give light to. *A lamp illuminated one corner of the dark room.*

im- a form of the prefix *in-* used before *m* or *p.*

im i tate /im ′ i tāt/ *v.* **im i tat ed, im i tat ing. 1.** to try to act or behave just as another person does; copy. **2.** to look like; resemble.

im me di ate /i mē ′ dē it/ *adj.* **1.** done or happening right away; without delay. **2.** close in time or space; near. —**im me di ate ly,** *adv.* —**im me di ate ness,** *n.*

im mense /i mens ′/ *adj.* of great size; very large; huge. —**im mense ly,** *adv.* —**im mense ness,** *n.*

im merse /i mûrs ′/ *v.* **im mersed, im mers ing. 1.** to cover completely by dipping into water or another liquid. **2.** to involve or occupy completely. *I was immersed in a good book.*

im par tial /im pär ′ shəl/ *adj.* not favoring one more than others; fair. *The judges of a contest should be impartial.* —**im par tial ly,** *adv.*

im pa tient /im pā ′ shənt/ *adj.* not able to put up with delay or opposition calmly and without anger. —**im pa tient ly,** *adv.*

im per son al /im pûr ′ sə nəl/ *adj.* **1.** not concerned with or referring to a particular person or persons; not personal. **2.** without emotion or feeling. —**im per son al ly,** *adv.*

im port /im pôrt ′, im ′ pôrt/ *v.* to bring in goods from another country for sale or use. —*n.* something that is imported.

im por tant /im pôr ′ tənt/ *adj.* **1.** having great value or meaning. **2.** having a high position or much power. **—im por tant ly,** *adv.*

im pose /im pōz ′/ *v.* **im posed, im pos ing. 1.** to put or set on a person. **2.** to make unfair or impolite demands. *I won't impose on you by taking your time.*

im pos si ble /im pos ′ ə bəl/ *adj.* not able to happen or be done. **—im pos si bly,** *adv.*

im prove /im prüv ′/ *v.* **im proved, im prov ing.** to make or become better. **—im prov a ble,** *adj.*

in- a prefix that means **1.** in, into, within, on, or toward. **2.** without; not.

in au gu rate /in ô ′ gyə rāt ′/ *v.* **in au gu rat ed, in au gu rat ing. 1.** to put a person in office with a formal ceremony. **2.** to open or begin to use formally. *The governor inaugurated the new bridge by driving across it.*

in ca pa ble /in kā ′ pə bəl/ *adj.* lacking the necessary power or skill to do something; not capable. **—in ca pa bil i ty,** *n.*

in clude /in klüd ′/ *v.* **in clud ed, in clud ing. 1.** to have as part of the whole; contain. **2.** to put in a group or total.

in con clu sive /in ′ kən klü ′ siv/ *adj.* that does not end argument or doubt. **—in con clu sive ly,** *adv.* **—in con clu sive ness,** *n.*

in cor rect /in ′ kə rekt ′/ *adj.* not right or correct; not proper **—in cor rect ly,** *adv.* **—in cor rect ness,** *n.*

in crease /in krēs ′, in ′ krēs/ *v.* **in creased, in creas ing.** to make or become larger in number or size. **—n.** an amount by which something is made larger.

in cred i ble /in kred ′ ə bəl/ *adj.* **1.** hard or impossible to believe. **2.** amazing; astonishing. **—in cred i bil i ty,** *n.* **—in cred i bly,** *adv.*

in debt ed /in det ′ id/ *adj.* **1.** owing money; in debt. *Until I pay back this loan, I am indebted to the bank.* **2.** owing gratitude to another for a favor. *I am indebted to you for all your help.*

in de pend ent /in ′ di pen ′ dənt/ *adj.* free from the control or rule of another or others; separate. **—in de pend ent ly,** *adv.*

in es cap a ble /in ′ e skā ′ pə bəl/ *adj.* that cannot be escaped or avoided; certain. *inescapable defeat.* **—in es cap a bly,** *adv.*

in fect /in fekt ′/ *v.* **1.** to spread a disease that is caused by a germ. **2.** to enter a living thing and cause disease. *Bacteria infected the cut on my hand.*

in fin i tive /in fin ′ i tiv/ *n.* a simple verb form. An infinitive is often preceded by the word "to." In the sentence "I like to swim," "to swim" is an infinitive.

in flate /in flāt ′/ *v.* **in flat ed, in flat ing.** to cause to swell by filling with air or gas. **—in fla tor,** *n.*

in flu ence /in ′ flü əns/ *n*. **1.** the power of a person or thing to produce an effect on others without using force or a command. **2.** a person or thing that has the power to produce an effect on others. —*v*. **in flu enced, in flu enc ing.** to have an effect on; especially by suggestions or serving as an example.

in form a tive /in fôr ′ mə tiv/ *adj*. giving information; instructive. *an informative book.*

in gre di ent /in grē ′ dē ənt/ *n*. any one of the parts that go into a mixture.

in hale /in hāl ′/ *v*. **in haled, in hal ing.** to take into the lungs; breathe in.

in hib it /in hib ′ it/ *v*. to hold back; check; restrain.

in ju ry /in ′ jə rē/ *n., pl.* **in ju ries.** harm or damage done to a person or thing.

in no cent /in ′ ə sənt/ *adj*. **1.** free from guilt or wrong. **2.** not doing harm; harmless. —**in no cent ly,** *adv*.

in sect /in ′ sekt ′/ *n*. any of a large group of small animals without a backbone. The body of an insect is divided into three parts. Insects have three pairs of legs and usually two pairs of wings. Flies, ants, grasshoppers, and beetles are insects.

in se cure /in ′ si kyür ′/ *adj*. **1.** likely to fail; not firm or stable. **2.** not safe from danger, harm, or loss. **3.** not

confident; fearful. *The student felt insecure before the start of the spelling contest.* —**in se cure ly,** *adv*.

in side /in ′ sīd ′, in sīd ′, in ′ sīd/ *n*. **1.** the inner side or part; interior. **2. insides.** the internal organs of the body. —*adj*. on or in the inside. *an inside seat on the train.* —*adv*. **1.** on, in, or into the inner side or part of within. *stepped inside the house.* **2.** indoors. —*prep*. in, into, or on the inner side or part of. *I looked inside the closet.*

in spi ra tion /in ′ spə rā ′ shən/ *n*. **1.** the stirring of the mind, feelings, or imagination, especially so that some good idea comes. **2.** a person or thing that stirs the mind, feelings, or imagination. **3.** a sudden, bright idea.

in spire /in spīr ′/ *v*. **in spired, in spir ing. 1.** to stir the mind, feelings, or imagination of. **2.** to fill with a strong, encouraging feeling. **3.** to move to action. *What inspired you to take up knitting?* —**in spir er,** *n*.

in stinct /in ′ stingkt ′/ *n*. a way of acting or behaving that a person or animal is born with and does not have to learn. *Birds build nests by instinct.*

in sti tu tion /in sti tü ′ shən, in ′ sti tū ′ shən/ *n*. **1.** an organization that is set up for a special purpose. *A school is an institution of learning.* **2.** a custom or practice that has been followed for a long time. —**in sti tu tion al,** *adj*.

adj. adjective
adv. adverb
conj. conjunction
contr. contraction
def. definition
interj. interjection
n. noun
pl. plural
prep. preposition
pron. pronoun
sing. singular
v. verb
v.i. intransitive verb
v.t. transitive verb

in struct /in strukt ′/ *v.* **1.** to show how to do or use something; teach. **2.** to give directions or orders to.

in te grate /in ′ ti grāt ′/ *v.* **in te grat ed, in te grat ing. 1.** to make open to people of all races. **2.** to bring parts together into a whole. *The reporter tried to integrate all the different accounts of the accident into one clear story.*

in te gra tion /in ′ ti grā ′ shən/ *n.* **1.** the act of making something open to people of all races. **2.** the act of bringing parts together into a whole.

in tel li gence /in tel ′ i jəns/ *n.* **1.** the ability to think, learn, and understand. **2.** information, especially about foreign countries or enemy forces. *The army's intelligence showed that the enemy was going to attack at dawn.*

in ter jec tion /in ′ tər jek ′ shən/ *n.* a word or phrase that shows strong feeling. An interjection can be used alone. "Oh!" and "Hey!" are interjections.

in ter rupt /in ′ tə rupt ′/ *v.* **1.** to break in upon or stop a person who is acting or speaking. **2.** to stop for a time; break off.

in ter rup tion /in ′ tə rup ′ shən/ *n.* **1.** the state of being interrupted. *There was an interruption in the radio program for a special report.* **2.** something that interrupts.

in trude /in trüd ′/ *v.* **in trud ed, in trud ing.** to come in as a disturbing or unwelcome addition; enter without being asked or wanted. **—in trud er,** *n.*

in va sion /in vā zhən/ *n.* **1.** the entrance of an army into a region in order to conquer it. **2.** a breaking into something without being asked or wanted.

in vent /in vent ′/ *v.* **1.** to make or think of for the first time; create. **2.** to make up. *I'm ashamed to say I invented an excuse for being late.*

in ven tion /in ven ′ chən/ *n.* **1.** the act of inventing. **2.** something that is invented. *Such inventions as the telephone and the computer have changed our way of life.*

in ves ti gate /in ves ′ ti gāt ′/ *v.* **in ves ti gat ed, in ves ti gat ing.** to look into carefully in order to find facts and get information.

in volve /in volv ′/ *v.* **in volved, in volv ing. 1.** to have as a necessary part; include. *This job involves a great deal of traveling.* **2.** to take up completely; absorb. *We were involved all day in household chores.* **—in volve ment,** *n.*

-ion a suffix used to form nouns from verbs that means **1.** the act of. **2.** the result of. **3.** the state of being.

/a/	at
/ā/	ape
/ä/	far
/â/	care
/e/	end
/ē/	me
/i/	it
/ī/	ice
/î/	pierce
/o/	hot
/ō/	old
/ô/	song
/ôr/	fork
/oi/	oil
/ou/	out
/u/	up
/ū/	use
/ü/	rule
/ù/	pull
/ûr/	turn
/ch/	chin
/ng/	sing
/sh/	shop
/th/	thin
/th/	this
/hw/	white
/zh/	treasure
/ə/	about
	taken
	pencil

lemon

Ire land /īr ′ lənd/ *n.* **1.** an island west of Great Britain that is divided into two countries, Ireland and Northern Ireland. **2.** the country called the **Republic of Ireland** in northwestern Europe, occupying most of the island of Ireland.

ir ra tion al /i rash ′ ə nəl/ *adj.* **1.** lacking reason. *The survivors of the crash wandered about in a confused and irrational state.* **2.** contrary to reason; illogical; absurd. **—ir ra tion al ly,** *adv.*

ir reg u lar /i reg ′ yə lər/ *adj.* **1.** not following a pattern; unequal or uneven in length, shape, or spacing. *irregular rows of trees.* **2.** not smooth; bumpy or rugged. **3.** not going by a rule, custom, or habit; unusual. **—ir reg u lar ly,** *adv.*

ir re spon si ble /ir ′ i spon ′ sə bəl/ *adj.* not trustworthy or reliable; not responsible. *It would be irresponsible to borrow a book and not return it.* **—ir re spon si bil i ty,** *n.* **—ir re spon si bly,** *adv.*

Is ra el /iz ′ rā əl, iz ′ rē əl/ *n.* a country in southwestern Asia at the eastern end of the Mediterranean.

-ist a suffix used to form nouns that means **1.** a person who does or makes something. **2.** a person who practices or has a profession.

-ity a suffix used to form nouns that means the state, condition, or quality of being.

adj.	adjective
adv.	adverb
conj.	conjunction
contr.	contraction
def.	definition
interj.	interjection
n.	noun
pl.	plural
prep.	preposition
pron.	pronoun
sing.	singular
v.	verb
v.i.	intransitive verb
v.t.	transitive verb

-ive a suffix used to form adjectives that means of; relating to; of the nature of.

jeal ous /jel ′ əs/ *adj.* **1.** fearful of losing someone's love to another person. **2.** having envy of a person or what a person has or can do. *I used to be jealous of my friend's ability to play football well.* **—jeal ous ly,** *adv.* **—jeal ous ness,** *n.*

jew el ry /jü ′ əl rē/ *n.* necklaces, pins, bracelets, or other ornaments. Jewelry is often decorated with precious stones.

jour ney /jûr ′ nē/ *n.* a long trip, **—***v.* to make a trip; travel.

judge /juj/ *v.* **judged, judg ing. 1.** to agree on a verdict or make a decision about a case in a court of law. **2.** to settle or decide. *to judge the dog show.* **—***n.* **1.** a person who decides on questions and disagreements in a court of law. **2.** a person who decides the winner in a contest or dispute. **3.** a person who knows enough about a subject to give an opinion about it. **—judg er,** *n.*

judg ment /juj ′ mənt/ *n.* **1.** the ability to decide or judge. **2.** an opinion. **3.** a verdict agreed on or a decision made by a court of law.

Ju pi ter /jü ′ pi tər/ *n.* the largest planet in our solar system. It is the fifth closest planet to the sun.

K

khak i /kak ′ ē, kä ′ kē/ *n.* **1.** a dull, yellowish-brown color. **2.** a heavy cotton cloth of this color. **3. khakis.** a military uniform or other clothing made from khaki.

kind ness /kīnd ′ nis/ *n., pl.* **kind ness es.** the quality or state of being kind or gentle, generous, and friendly.

knead /nēd/ *v.* to mix and press together with the hands. *The baker had to knead the dough before baking it.* —**knead er,** *n.*

kneel /nēl/ *v.* to go down on a bent knee or knees. —**kneel er,** *n.*

knelt /nelt/ *v.* A past tense and past participle of *kneel.*

know /nō/ *v.* **knew, known, know ing. 1.** to understand clearly; be certain of the facts or truth of. **2.** to be acquainted or familiar with. **3.** to have skill or experience with.

knowl edge /nol ′ ij/ *n.* **1.** an understanding that is gained through experience or study. **2.** the fact of knowing.

known /nōn/ *v.* past participle of

know. *A great deal is known about the harmful effects of pollution.*

knuck le /nuk ′ əl/ *n.* a joint in the finger. —*v.* **knuck led, knuck ling.** to press, rub, or hit with the knuckles.

L

la goon /lə gün ′/ *n.* a shallow body of water usually connected to a larger body of water.

launch [1] /lônch/ *n., pl.* **launch es.** an open motorboat.

launch [2] /lonch/ *v.* **1.** to start in motion; send off. **2.** to put into the water.

laun dro mat /lôn drə mat ′/ *n.* a laundry where people can wash their own clothes. It has washing machines and clothes dryers that work when coins are put in them.

laun dry /lôn ′ drē/ *n., pl.* **laun dries. 1.** clothes and linens that are to be or have been washed. **2.** a place where clothes, sheets, and other things are washed.

lei sure /lē ′ zhər, lezh ′ ər/ *n.* the time to do what one likes; free time.

lodge /loj/ *n.* **1.** a small house, cottage, or cabin. **2.** a branch of a club or other organization. —*v.* **lodged, lodg ing. 1.** to live in a place for a while. **2.** to provide with a place to live for a while; rent rooms to. **3.** to become stuck or fixed in a place. *A pebble lodged in my shoe.*

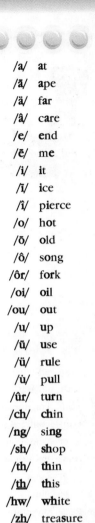

/a/	at
/ā/	ape
/ä/	far
/â/	care
/e/	end
/ē/	me
/i/	it
/ī/	ice
/î/	pierce
/o/	hot
/ō/	old
/ô/	song
/ôr/	fork
/oi/	oil
/ou/	out
/u/	up
/ū/	use
/ü/	rule
/ù/	pull
/ûr/	turn
/ch/	chin
/ng/	sing
/sh/	shop
/th/	thin
/th/	this
/hw/	white
/zh/	treasure
/ə/	about
	taken
	pencil
	lemon

lone li ness /lōn ′ lē nis/ *n.* the state of being lonely.

lone ly /lōn ′ lē/ *adj.* **lone li er, lone li est. 1.** unhappy from being alone. **2.** away from others; alone. **3.** not often visited or used by people; deserted. *We were the only people on the lonely beach.*

loose /lüs/ *adj.* **loos er, loos est. 1.** not fastened or attached firmly. **2.** free. **3.** not tight. —*v.* **loosed, loos ing. 1.** to set free; let go. **2.** to make or become less tight; loosen or unfasten. —**loose ly,** *adv.* —**loose ness,** *n.*

lose /lüz/ *v.* **lost, los ing. 1.** to have no longer; be without. **2.** to fail to keep. *Do you lose your temper easily?* **3.** to fail to win.

lug gage /lug ′ ij/ *n.* the suitcases, trunks, and bags that a traveler takes along on a trip; baggage.

M

mag nif i cent /mag nif ′ ə sənt/ *adj.* very beautiful and grand; splendid. —**mag nif i cent ly,** *adv.*

main tain /mān tān ′/ *v.* **1.** to continue to have or do; go on with; keep. **2.** to take care of.

ma jor i ty /mə jôr ′ i tē, mə jor ′ i tē/ *n.,* *pl.* **ma jor i ties.** the larger number or part of something; more than half.

man age ment /man ′ ij mənt/ *n.* **1.** the act or process of directing or controlling. *The business failed because of bad management.* **2.** the person or persons who manage something, such as a business.

man a ger /man ′ i jər/ *n.* a person who manages something. *The manager of the baseball team decided which player would pitch.*

Mars /märz/ *n.* the seventh largest planet in our solar system. It is the fourth planet in order of distance from the sun.

mar vel ous /mär ′ və ləs/ *adj.* **1.** causing wonder or amazement. **2.** outstanding; excellent.

math e mat ics /math ə mat ′ iks/ *n.* the study of numbers, quantities, measurements, and shapes, and how they relate to each other.

ma ture /mə chür ′, mə tür ′, mə tyür ′/ *adj.* have reached full growth or development; ripe.

ma tu ri ty /mə chür ′ i tē, mə tür ′ i tē, mə tyür ′ i tē/ *n.* the state or quality of being mature.

meas ure ment /mezh ′ ər mənt/ *n.* **1.** the act of measuring. *Rulers and scales are used for measurement.* **2.** something found or shown by measuring; the size, height, or amount of something.

me chan ic /mi kan ′ ik/ *n.* a person who is skilled in repairing and operating machines.

mem o ry /mem ′ ə rē/ *n., pl.*
mem o ries. 1. the ability to remember things. **2.** a person or thing that is remembered. **3.** all that a person can remember. *The student recited the poem from memory.*

-ment a suffix that means **1.** the act of **2.** the result or product of. *Improvement* is the result of improving.

Mer cu ry /mûr ′ kyə rē/ *n.* the second smallest planet in our solar system. It is the closest planet to the sun.

mes sen ger /mes ′ ən jər/ *n.* a person who delivers messages or runs errands.

met ric /met ′ rik/ *adj.* of or having to do with the metric system. *The gram is a metric measurement.*

Mex i co /mek ′ si kō/ *n.* a country in North America, south of the United States.

mi cro phone /mī ′ krə fōn/ *n.* a device that is used to transmit sound or to make it louder.

might y /mī ′ tē/ *adj.* **might i er, might i est.** great in power, size, or amount. *The Pacific is a mighty ocean.*—**might i ness,** *n.*

mi grate /mī ′ grāt/ *v.* **mi grat ed, mi grat ing.** to move from one place to another. *Many birds migrate to the south in the fall.*

mil li me ter /mil ′ ə mē tər/ *n.* a unit of length in the metric system. A mil-

limeter is equal to one thousandth of a meter, or about .039 of an inch.

mil lion /mil ′ yən/ *n.* **1.** one thousand times one thousand; 1,000,000. **2.** a very large number. *It looks like there are a million stars in the sky tonight.*

min ute /min ′ it/ *n.* **1.** a unit of time equal to sixty seconds. **2.** a moment in time; instant. **3. minutes.** a written report of what was said and done at a meeting.

mi rac u lous /mi rak ′ yə ləs/ *adj.* **1.** impossible to explain by the laws of nature. **2.** amazing; marvelous. —**mi rac u lous ly,** *adv.* —**mi rac u lous ness,** *n.*

mis chie vous /mis ′ chə vəs/ *adj.* **1.** full of mischief; playful but naughty. **2.** causing trouble; harmful. *The candidate was hurt by the mischievous rumors being spread by opponents.* —**mis chie vous ly,** *adv.* —**mis chie vous ness,** *n.*

mis judge /mis juj ′/ *v.* **mis judged, mis judg ing.** to judge wrongly or unfairly. —**mis judg ment;** *also,* **mis judge ment,** *n.*

mis lay /mis lā ′/ *v.* **mis laid, mis lay ing.** to put in a place that is later forgotten. *I mislaid my skates and couldn't find them.*

mis match /mis mach ′, mis ′ mach ′/ *v.* to match or join together unwisely or unsuitably. —*n., pl.* **mis match es.** an unwise or unsuitable match.

mis spell /mis spel ′/ *v.* **mis spelled** or **mis spelt** /mis spelt ′/, **mis spell ing.** to spell a word incorrectly.

/a/ at
/ā/ ape
/ä/ far
/â/ care
/e/ end
/ē/ me
/i/ it
/ī/ ice
/î/ pierce
/o/ hot
/ō/ old
/ô/ song
/ôr/ fork
/oi/ oil
/ou/ out
/u/ up
/ū/ use
/ü/ rule
/ů/ pull
/ûr/ turn
/ch/ chin
/ng/ sing
/sh/ shop
/th/ thin
/th/ this
/hw/ white
/zh/ treasure
/ə/ about
taken
pencil

lemon

moc ca sin /mok ′ ə sin/ *n.* a soft leather shoe or slipper with no heel. Moccasins were first worn by American Indians.

mon ar chy /mon ′ ər kē/ *n., pl.* **mon ar chies. 1.** government by a king, queen, or other monarch. **2.** a nation or state that is ruled by a monarch.

mon i tor /mon ′ i tər/ *n.* **1.** a student who is given a special duty to do. **2.** any person who warns or keeps watch. **3.** the screen that a computer uses to display numbers, letters, and pictures. It is similar to a television screen. —*v.* to watch over or observe something.

adj. adjective
adv. adverb
conj. conjunction
contr. contraction
def. definition
interj. interjection
n. noun
pl. plural
prep. preposition
pron. pronoun
sing. singular
v. verb
v.i. intransitive verb
v.t. transitive verb

mono- a prefix that means one; single; alone.

mo nop o lize /mə nop ′ ə līz ′/ *v.* **mo nop o lized, mo nop o liz ing. 1.** to get or have a monopoly of. **2.** to get, have, or use all of. *Don't monopolize the teacher's attention.*

mo nop o ly /mə nop ′ ə lē/ *n., pl.* **mo nop o lies. 1.** the sole control of a product or service by a person or company. *That bus company has a monopoly on public transportation in our town.* **2.** a person or company that has such control.

mon o rail /mon ′ ə rāl ′/ *n.* **1.** a train or other vehicle that runs on or is suspended from a single rail. **2.** a railroad track that has only one rail instead of two.

mon o tone /mon ′ ə tōn ′/ *n.* speech or vocal sound uttered with no change in tone. *The announcer's dull monotone made the program very boring.*

mos qui to /mə skē ′ tō/ *n., pl.* **mos qui toes** or **mos qui tos.** a small insect with two wings. The female gives a sting or bite that itches. Some mosquitoes carry malaria and other diseases.

moun tain /moun ′ tən/ *n.* **1.** a mass of land that rises very high above the surrounding area. **2.** a very large pile or amount of something. *mountains of trash.*

moun tain ous /moun ′ tə nəs/ *adj.* **1.** having many mountains. **2.** very big; huge.

mul ti pli ca tion /mul ′ tə pli kā ′ shən/ *n.* the mathematical operation of taking a number and adding it to itself a certain number of times. In the multiplication of 2 times 4, you are adding 2 sets of 4, which equals 8.

mur mur /mûr ′ mər/ *n.* a low, soft sound. *the murmur of the brook.* —*v.* to make or say with a low, soft sound. —**mur mur er,** *n.*

mu se um /mū zē ′ əm/ *n.* a building where objects of art, science, or history are kept and displayed for people to see.

my thol o gy /mi thol ′ ə jē/ *n., pl.* **my thol o gies.** a group or collection of myths and legends. *All the myths that were told and written in ancient Greece are known as Greek mythology.*

na tion al i ty /nash ′ ə nal ′ i tē/ *n., pl.* **na tion al i ties. 1.** the fact or condition of belonging to a particular nation. **2.** a group of people who share the same language, culture, and history.

ne ces si ty /ni ses ′ i tē/ *n., pl.* **nec ces si ties. 1.** something that cannot be done without; requirement. **2.** the fact of being necessary.

Nep tune /nep ′ tün, nep ′ tūn/ *n.* the fourth largest planet in our solar system. It is the eighth planet in order of distance from the sun. Neptune can be seen from earth only with the aid of a telescope.

nerv ous /nûr ′ vəs/ *adj.* **1.** not able to relax; tense. *Loud noises make me nervous.* **2.** fearful or timid. **—nerv ous ly,** *adv.* **—nerv ous ness,** *n.*

-ness a suffix that means the quality, state, or condition of being.

neu tral /nü ′ trəl, nū ′ trəl/ *adj.* not taking or belonging to either side in a conflict. **—neu tral ly,** *adv.*

neu tral i ty /nü tral ′ i tē, nū tral ′ i tē/ *n.* the quality or state of being neutral. *The country maintained its neutrality throughout the war.*

niece /nēs/ *n.* **1.** the daughter of one's brother or sister. **2.** the daughter of one's brother-in-law or sister-in-law.

nine ty /nīn ′ tē/ *n., pl.* **nine ties.** nine times ten; 90.

non prof it /non prof ′ it/ *adj.* not operated for profit. *a nonprofit hospital.*

non sense /non ′ sens/ *n.* **1.** a way of talking or acting that is silly and makes no sense. **2.** language or behavior that is annoying or lacking in good sense.

non stan dard /non stan ′ dərd/ *adj.* **1.** of or relating to usage or language that is not considered acceptable by educated users of the language. **2.** not standard.

non vi o lence /non vī ′ ə ləns/ *n.* the philosophy or practice of opposing the use of all physical force or violence. **—non vi o lent,** *adj.* **—non vi o lent ly,** *adv.*

nor mal /nôr ′ məl/ *adj.* conforming to a standard, pattern, or model; regular; usual.

no tice /nō ′ tis/ *n.* **1.** the condition of being seen or observed. **2.** a warning or announcement. **3.** a printed or written announcement. **—v. no ticed, no tic ing.** to become aware of; observe.

nui sance /nü ′ səns, nū ′ səns/ *n.* a person, thing, or action that annoys or offends.

/a/	at
/ā/	ape
/ä/	far
/â/	care
/e/	end
/ē/	me
/i/	it
/ī/	ice
/î/	pierce
/o/	hot
/ō/	old
/ô/	song
/ôr/	fork
/oi/	oil
/ou/	out
/u/	up
/ū/	use
/ü/	rule
/ù/	pull
/ûr/	turn
/ch/	chin
/ng/	sing
/sh/	shop
/th/	thin
/th/	this
/hw/	white
/zh/	treasure
/ə/	about
	taken
	pencil
	lemon

num ber /num ′ bər/ *n.* **1.** the total amount of things in a group; how many there are of something. **2.** a symbol or word that tells how many or which one. **3.** a total or sum. —*v.* **1.** to find out the number of; count. **2.** to give a number or numbers to. **3.** to amount to or include; contain.

nu mer a tor /nü ′ mə rā tər, nū ′ mə rā′ tər/ *n.* the number above or to the left of the line in a fraction. In the fraction 1/2, 1 is the numerator and 2 is the denominator.

nu mer ous /nü ′ mər əs, nū ′ mər əs/ *adj.* **1.** forming a large number; many. **2.** containing a large number; large. —**nu mer ous ly,** *adv.* —**nu mer ous ness,** *n.*

oc ca sion /ə kā ′ zhən/ *n.* **1.** the time when something happens. **2.** an important or special event.

oc cu pa tion /ok ′ yə pā ′ shən/ *n.* **1.** the work a person does in order to earn a living; profession. **2.** the act of occupying or the condition of being occupied. *The enemy soldiers' occupation of the town lasted for months.*

oc cur rence /ə kûr ′ əns/ *n.* something that takes place or happens. *Rain is an unusual occurrence in the desert.*

o cean /ō ′ shən/ *n.* **1.** the whole body of salt water that covers nearly three fourths of the earth's surface. **2.** any one of the four main parts of this body of water: the Atlantic, Pacific, Indian, or Arctic Ocean.

op por tu ni ty /op ′ ər tü ′ ni tē, op ər tū ′ ni tē/ *n., pl.* **op por tu ni ties.** a good chance; favorable time.

op ti mum /op ′ tə məm/ *n., pl.* **op ti ma** /op ′ tə mə/ or **optimums.** the best, highest possible, or most favorable point or level. —*adj.* best, highest possible, or most favorable.

or bit /ôr ′ bit/ *n.* **1.** the path that a planet or other heavenly body follows as it moves in a circle around another heavenly body. **2.** one complete trip of a spacecraft along such a path. —*v.* to move in an orbit around a heavenly body.

or ches tra /ôr ′ kə strə/ *n.* **1.** a group of musicians playing together on various instruments. **2.** the violins, horns, drums, and other instruments played by such a group. **3.** the area just in front of a stage in which the orchestra plays.

or di nar y /ôr ′ də ner ′ ē/ *adj.* **1.** commonly used; regular; usual. **2.** not different in any way from others; average. —**or di nar i ness,** *n.*

or gan ize /ôr ′ gə nīz ′/ *v.* **or gan ized, or gan iz ing.** to arrange or put together in an orderly way. **2.** to cause to join together in a labor union or other organization. —**or gan iz a ble,** *adj.* —**or gan iz er,** *n.*

or i gin /ôr ′ i jin, or ′ i jin/ *n.* the cause or source of something; what something begins or comes from. *The origin of the fire was in the basement.*

or na ment /ôr ′ nə mənt/ *n.* something that is used as a decoration. /ôr ′ nə ment/—*v.* to decorate with ornaments. —**or na men ta tion,** *n.*

out- a prefix that means **1.** outside or outward. **2.** more than or better than.

out stand ing /out stan ′ ding/ *adj.* so good as to stand out from others of its kind. *an outstanding book report.* —**out stand ing ly,** *adv.*

o ver whelm /ō ′ vər hwelm ′, ō ′ vər welm ′/ *v.* to overcome completely; overpower or make helpless. *The enemy overwhelmed our soldiers.*—**o ver whelm ing ly,** *adv.*

ox /oks/ *n., pl.* **ox en.** the adult male of domesticated cattle.

Pa ki stan /pak ′ ə stan ′/ *n.* a country in south-central Asia.

par a graph /par ′ ə graf ′/ *n.* a part of something written, made up of one or more sentences about a particular subject or idea. It begins on a new line that is indented from the rest of the lines.

par al lel /par ′ ə lel/ *adj.* being the same distance apart at all points. If lines are parallel, they never meet or cross each other.

par cel /pär ′ səl/ *n.* something wrapped up; bundle or package. —*v.* to divide into sections; give out in parts.

par don /pär ′ dən/ *v.* to free a person from punishment. —*v.* the act of refusing to blame or punish; forgiveness. —**par don a ble,** *adj.* —**par don a bly,** *adv.* —**par don er,** *n.*

par ent /pâr ′ ənt/ *n.* **1.** a father or mother. **2.** a living thing, as an animal or plant, that has produced offspring.

par tial /pär ′ shəl/ *n.* **1.** not complete; not total. **2.** showing more favor than is fair to one side, person, or group. —**par tial ly,** *adv.*

par ti ci ple /pär ′ tə sip ′ əl/ *n.* a form of a verb that is used with a helping verb to form certain tenses. A participle also can act as a noun or adjective. In the sentence "I am going to the movies now that my homework is finished," the words "going" and "finished" are participles.

pas sen ger /pas ′ ən jər/ *n.* a person who travels in an automobile, bus, airplane, or other vehicle.

pa tience /pā ′ shəns/ *n.* the quality or fact of being able to put up with hardship, pain, trouble, or delay without getting angry or upset.

pe cul iar /pi kül ′ yər/ *adj.* **1.** not usual; strange. **2.** belonging to a certain person, group, place, or thing. *The kangaroo is peculiar to Australia and New Guinea.* —**pe cul iar ly,** *adv.*

pen ni less /pen ′ ē lis/ *adj.* having no money at all. *After paying all my bills, I was penniless.* —**pen ni less ness,** *n.*

/a/	at
/ā/	ape
/ä/	far
/â/	care
/e/	end
/ē/	me
/i/	it
/ī/	ice
/î/	pierce
/o/	hot
/ō/	old
/ô/	song
/ôr/	fork
/oi/	oil
/ou/	out
/u/	up
/ū/	use
/ü/	rule
/ù/	pull
/ûr/	turn
/ch/	chin
/ng/	sing
/sh/	shop
/th/	thin
/th/	this
/hw/	white
/zh/	treasure
/ə/	about
	taken
	pencil
	lemon

peo ple /pē ′ pəl/ *n.*, *pl.* **peo ple.** men, women, and children; persons. —*v.* **peo pled, peo pling.** to fill with people; inhabit. *A great number of human beings people the earth.*

per form er /pər fôr ′ mər/ *n.* a person who sings, acts, or does some form of entertainment in public.

pe rim e ter /pə rim ′ i tər/ *n.* the boundary of a figure or an area. *The perimeter of a square is equal to four times the length of one side.*

pe ri od /pîr ′ ē əd/ *n.* **1.** a portion of time. **2.** a punctuation mark (.) used at the end of a declarative sentence or an imperative sentence or at the end of an abbreviation.

adj.	adjective
adv.	adverb
conj.	conjunction
contr.	contraction
def.	definition
interj.	interjection
n.	noun
pl.	plural
prep.	preposition
pron.	pronoun
sing.	singular
v.	verb
v.i.	intransitive verb
v.t.	transitive verb

per ma nent /pûr ′ mə nənt/ *adj.* lasting or meant to last; enduring. —**per ma nent ly,** *adv.*

per mis sion /pər mish ′ ən/ *n.* a consent from someone in authority.

per pet u al /pər pech ′ ü əl/ *adj.* **1.** lasting for a very long time or forever. **2.** continuing without stopping. *The perpetual rise and fall of the tides is influenced by the moon and sun.* —**per pet u al ly,** *adv.*

Phil ip pines /fil ′ ə pēnz ′, fil ′ ə pēnz ′/ *n.* a country that is a group of islands in southeastern Asia.

phrase /frāz/ *n.* a group of words that expresses a thought but does not contain both a subject and a predicate. In the sentence "We walked to town," "to town" is a phrase. —*v.* **phrased, phras ing.** to express in chosen words.

plan et /plan ′ it/ *n.* one of nine large heavenly bodies that orbit the sun. The planets in our solar system are Mercury, Venus, Earth, Mars, Jupiter, Saturn, Uranus, Neptune, and Pluto.

plumb er /plum ′ ər/ *n.* a person who puts in and repairs water and sewage pipes in buildings.

Plu to /plü ′ tō/ *n.* the smallest planet in our solar system. It is the planet farthest from the sun. Pluto can be seen from earth only with the aid of a telescope.

pop u lar /pop ′ yə lər/ *adj.* **1.** liked or accepted by many people. **2.** having many friends; liked by many. —**pop u lar ly,** *adv.*

pop u lar i ty /pop ′ yə lar ′ i tē/ *n.* the condition of being popular.

pos ses sion /pə zesh ′ ən/ *n.* **1.** the act or condition of having or owning something. **2.** something owned. *The family lost their possessions in the fire.*

pos si ble /pos ′ ə bəl/ *adj.* **1.** capable of being, being done, or happening. **2.** capable of being used or considered.

praise wor thy /prāz ′ wûr ′ <u>th</u>ē/ *adj.* worthy of praise; commendable. —**praise wor thi ly,** *adv.* —**praise wor thi ness,** *n.*

pre ar range /prē ′ ə ranj ′/ *v.*
pre ar ranged, pre ar rang ing. to
arrange beforehand.
—**pre ar range ment,** *n.*

pre cau tion /pri kô ′ shən/ *n.* something done beforehand to prevent
harm or danger. *Looking both ways is
a good precaution to take before
crossing the street.*

prec e dent /pres ′ i dənt, pri sē ′ dənt/
n. an action or decision that may
serve as an example to be followed in
the future. *The decision of the court
set a precedent for how similar cases
would be settled.*

pred i cate /pred ′ i kit/ *n.* a word or
group of words in a sentence that
tells what the subject does or what is
done to the subject. The predicate
may also give some descriptive information about the subject. In the sentence "Because of the rain our car
skidded," the verb "skidded" is the
predicate.

pre dict /pri dikt ′/ *v.* to tell beforehand. —**pre dict a ble,** *adj.*

pref ace /pref ′ is/ *n.* an introduction
to a book or speech.

pre fix /prē ′ fiks ′/ *n., pl.* **pre fix es.** a
syllable or group of syllables that is
added to the beginning of a word or
root to change the meaning and form
a new word. The word *dislike* is
made up of the prefix *dis* and the
word *like.*

pre his tor ic /prē ′ his tôr ′ ik,
prē ′ his tor ′ ik/ *adj.* belonging to a
time before people started writing
history. *Dinosaurs were prehistoric
animals.* —**pre his tor i cal ly,** *adv.*

pre ma ture /prē ′ mə chur ′,
prē ′ mə tyùr ′, prē ′ mə tùr ′/ *adj.*
arriving, happening, existing, or
done before the usual or proper time;
too early or too soon. *a premature
decision.* —**pre ma ture ly,** *adv.*
—**pre ma ture ness,** *n.*

pre mo ni tion /prē ′ mə nish ′ ən,
prem ′ ə nish ′ ən/ *n.* a feeling that
something is about to happen, especially something bad or harmful.

pre oc cu pied /prē ok ′ yə pīd ′/ *adj.*
absorbed in thought; engrossed.

prep a ra tion /prep ′ ə rā ′ shən/ *n.*
the act of making something ready,
or the condition of being made
ready.

pre pare /pri pâr ′/ *v.* **pre pared,
pre par ing.** to make or get ready.
—**pre par er,** *n.*

prep o si tion /prep ′ ə zish ′ ən/ *n.* a
word that shows the relation between
another word and a noun or pronoun. In the sentence "The neighbors
across the street never argue with
us," the words "across" and "with" are
prepositions.

pre scribe /pri skrīb ′/ *v.* **pre scribed,
pre scrib ing.** to order for use as a
medical treatment. *The doctor pre-
scribed an ointment for my rash.*

pres ence /prez ′ əns/ *n.* the fact of
being in a place at a certain time. *The
presence of the growling dog in the
room made me nervous.*

/a/	at
/ā/	ape
/ä/	far
/â/	care
/e/	end
/ē/	me
/i/	it
/ī/	ice
/î/	pierce
/o/	hot
/ō/	old
/ô/	song
/ôr/	fork
/oi/	oil
/ou/	out
/u/	up
/ū/	use
/ü/	rule
/ù/	pull
/ûr/	turn
/ch/	chin
/ng/	sing
/sh/	shop
/th/	thin
/<u>th</u>/	this
/hw/	white
/zh/	treasure
/ə/	about
	taken
	pencil
	lemon

173

pres sure /presh ′ ər/ *n.* **1.** force caused by one thing pushing against another thing. *The pressure of the driver's foot on the gas pedal made the car go faster.* **2.** strong influence or persuasion. —*v.* **pres sured, pres sur ing.** to urge strongly.

pre view /prē ′ vū/ *n.* a showing of something ahead of time.

pre vi ous /prē ′ vē əs/ *adj.* coming before; earlier. —**pre vi ous ly,** *adv.*

prob a bil i ty /prob ′ ə bil ′ i tē/ *n., pl.* **prob a bil i ties. 1.** the chances of something happening; likelihood. **2.** a thing that is likely to happen.

pro ce dure /prə sē ′ jər/ *n.* a proper way of doing something, usually by a series of steps. —**pro ce du ral,** *adj.*

pro ces sion /prə sesh ′ ən/ *n.* **1.** a continuous forward movement of something or someone. **2.** a group of persons moving forward in a line in a certain order.

proc la ma tion /prok ′ lə mā ′ shən/ *n.* an official announcement of something. *Abraham Lincoln made a proclamation in 1863 that freed slaves in many states.*

prod uct /prod ′ əkt/ *n.* **1.** anything that is made or created. **2.** a number that is gotten by multiplying two other numbers. *When you multiply 3 times 4, the product is 12.*

prog ress /prog ′ res, prə gres ′/ *n.* a forward movement. —*v.* to move forward. *The building of the new house progressed rapidly.*

pro jec tion /prə jek ′ shən/ *n.* **1.** the act of throwing something forward. **2.** the picture or other image that is projected onto a screen or other surface. **3.** a prediction that is based on certain information. **4.** something that sticks out or projects.

prom i nent /prom ′ ə nənt/ *adj.* **1.** well-known or important. **2.** very easy to see because it stands out in some way; noticeable. —**prom i nent ly,** *adv.*

pro mo tion /prə mō ′ shən/ *n.* the change to a higher rank, position, or grade. *She got a promotion to manager.* —**pro mo tion al,** *adj.*

pro noun /prō ′ noun/ *n.* a word that takes the place of one or more nouns or noun phrases. In the sentence "We gave it to them yesterday," "We," "it," and "them" are pronouns.

pro nounce /prə nouns ′/ *v.* **pro nounced, pro nounc ing. 1.** to make the sound of a letter or word. **2.** to say or declare. *The judge pronounced the prisoner not guilty.* **pro nounce a ble,** *adj.*

pro pel lant /prə pel ′ ənt/ *n.* a propelling agent or substance, especially a fuel for propelling a rocket.

pro per /prop ′ ər/ *adj.* correct or suitable for a certain purpose or occasion.

pro pose /prə pōs ′/ *v.* **pro posed, pro pos ing. 1.** to suggest something or someone to other people for their consideration. **2.** to intend or plan to do something. **3.** to make an offer of marriage.

pro tec tive /prə tek ′ tiv/ *adj.* keeping from harm; protecting.

pro voke /prə vōk ′/ *v.* **pro voked, pro vok ing. 1.** to make angry. **2.** to stir; excite. **3.** to bring out; arouse. *The newspaper article provoked discussion.* —**pro vok ing ly,** *adv.*

pub lish /pub ′ lish/ *v.* to print a newspaper, magazine, book, or other material and offer it for sale.

pud ding /pùd ′ ing/ *n.* a sweet, soft dessert that is cooked.

punc tu a tion /pungk ′ chü ā ′ shən/ *n.* the use of periods, commas, and other punctuation marks to make the meaning of written material clear.

quar an tine /kwôr ′ ən tēn ′, kwor ′ ən tēn ′/ *n.* the keeping of a person, animal, or thing away from others to stop the spreading of a disease. —*v.* **quar an tined, quar an tin ing.** to put a person or thing in quarantine.

quest /kwest/ *n.* a search or pursuit. *The explorers went in quest of gold.*

ques tion /kwes ′ chən/ *n.* **1.** something asked in order to get an answer or find out something. **2.** a matter to be talked over. —*v.* **1.** to ask questions of or about. **2.** to express doubt about. *I question the truth of your story.*

quo tient /kwō ′ shənt/ *n.* a number obtained by dividing one number by another. *If you divide 12 by 4, the quotient is 3.*

rap id /rap ′ id/ *adj.* very quick; fast. *The train went at a rapid pace.* —**rap id ly,** *adv.* —**rap id ness,** *n.*

re- a prefix that means again. *Reprint* means to print again.

re ac tion /rē ak ′ shən/ *n.* an action in response to something that has happened or has been done.

re al ize /rē ′ ə līz ′/ *v.,* **re a lized, re al iz ing. 1.** to understand completely. **2.** to make real. *Years of saving money helped us to realize our dream of owning a house.*

re ceipt /ri sēt ′/ *n.* a written statement showing that a package, mail, or money has been received.

re ceive /ri sēv ′/ *v.* **re ceived, re ceiv ing.** to take or get.

re cent /rē ′ sənt/ *adj.* done, made, or happening not long ago. —**re cent ly,** *adv.* —**re cent ness,** *n.*

rec om mend /rek ′ ə mend ′/ *v.* **1.** to speak in favor of. **2.** to advise; suggest. **3.** to make acceptable or pleasing. *Your excellent skills recommend you for this job.*

/a/	at
/ā/	ape
/ä/	far
/â/	care
/e/	end
/ē/	me
/i/	it
/ī/	ice
/î/	pierce
/o/	hot
/ō/	old
/ô/	song
/ôr/	fork
/oi/	oil
/ou/	out
/u/	up
/ū/	use
/ü/	rule
/ù/	pull
/ûr/	turn
/ch/	chin
/ng/	sing
/sh/	shop
/th/	thin
/ṯh/	this
/hw/	white
/zh/	treasure
/ə/	about
	taken
	pencil
	lemon
	circus

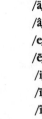

175

rec om men da tion
/rek ′ ə men dā ′ shən/ *n.* **1.** the act of recommending. *Your recommendation of the movie makes me want to see it.* **2.** something recommended; advice; suggestion.

rec re a tion /rek ′ rē ā ′ shən/ *n.* something that is done for amusement or relaxation. *Sports, games, and hobbies are kinds of recreation.*

rec tan gle /rek ′ tang gəl/ *n.* a figure with four sides that has four right angles. *A square is a rectangle whose four sides are equal.*

re en try /rē en ′ trē/ *n., pl.* **re en tries.** **1.** an entering again. **2.** the return of a spacecraft or missile from space into the earth's atmosphere.

re fresh ment /ri fresh ′ mənt/ *n.* **1.** food or drink. **2.** a refreshing or being refreshed. *I needed refreshment after working hard all day.*

re lease /ri lēs ′/ *v.* **re leased, re leas ing.** **1.** to set free; let go. **2.** to allow to be seen, published, or broadcast. —*n.* the act of releasing or the state of being released.

re luc tance /ri luk ′ təns/ *n.* the state of being reluctant; lack of eagerness; hesitation or unwillingness.

re main der /ri mān ′ dər/ *n.* **1.** a remaining part. **2.** the number found when one number is subtracted from another. **3.** the number left over when a number cannot be divided evenly. *If you divide 3 into 10, the answer is 3 with a remainder of 1.*

re mark a ble /ri mär ′ kə bəl/ *adj.* worthy of being noticed; not ordinary; unusual. *Your science project is remarkable.* —**re mark a ble ness,** *n.* —**re mark a bly,** *adv.*

re mind er /ri mīn ′ dər/ *n.* something that makes someone remember.

re ply /ri plī ′/ *v.* **re plied, re ply ing.** to answer in speech, writing, or action. —*n., pl.* **re plies.** something said, written, or done in answer.

res er va tion /rez ′ ər vā ′ shən/ *n.* **1.** an arrangement to have something kept for a particular person or persons. **2.** land set aside by the government for a special purpose.

res i dent /rez ′ i dənt/ *n.* a person who lives in a particular place. *They are residents of this town.*

re sist ance /ri zis ′ təns/ *n.* **1.** the act of resisting. *The soldiers could not put up much resistance to the enemy.* **2.** the ability to overcome something. **3.** a force that opposes or works against the motion of another.

res tau rant /res ′ tər ənt, res ′ tə ränt ′/ *n.* a place where food is prepared and served to customers.

re view /ri vū ′/ *v.* **1.** to study, go over, or examine again. **2.** to go over in one's mind; look back on. **3.** to give a critical account of. —*n.* **1.** a studying, going over, or examining again. **2.** a looking back. **3.** an account of a movie, play, book, or other work given to praise or criticize it.

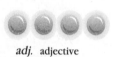

adj.	adjective
adv.	adverb
conj.	conjunction
contr.	contraction
def.	definition
interj.	interjection
n.	noun
pl.	plural
prep.	preposition
pron.	pronoun
sing.	singular
v.	verb
v.i.	intransitive verb
v.t.	transitive verb

rhine stone /rīn ′ stōn/ *n.* a colorless cut gem made of quartz or glass paste, used to imitate diamonds.

rhi noc er os /rī nos ′ ər əs/ *n., pl.* **rhi noc er os es** or **rhi noc er os.** a very large animal having thick skin and one or two horns rising from the snout. Rhinoceroses live in open, grassy areas of Africa and Asia.

rhom bus /rom ′ bəs/ *n., pl.* **rhom bus es** or **rhom bi.** a flat figure with four sides of equal length. The opposite sides of a rhombus are parallel.

ri dic u lous /ri dik ′ yə ləs/ *adj.* very silly or foolish. **—ri dic u lous ly,** *adv.* **—ri dic u lous ness,** *n.*

ro de o /rō ′ dē ō , rō dā ′ ō/ *n., pl.* **ro de os.** a show with contests in horseback riding, roping, and other similar skills.

rou tine /rü tēn ′/ *n.* **1.** a regular way of doing something. **2.** sameness of actions or ways of doing things. *—adj.* according to or using routine; regular. **—rou tine ly,** *adv.*

rub bish /rub ′ ish/ *n.* **1.** useless waste material; trash. **2.** worthless talk or thoughts; nonsense.

sac ri fice /sak ′ rə fīs ′/ *n.* **1.** the ceremony of offering something to God or a god as an act of worship. **2.** the giving up of something that is want-ed. *—v.* **sac ri ficed, sac ri ficing. 1.** to offer as a sacrifice to God or a god. **2.** to give up for the sake of someone else or something else.

salm on /sam ′ ən/ *n., pl.* **salm on** or **salm ons. 1.** a large fish with a silver-colored body. **2.** a yellowish pink color *—adj.* having the color salmon.

sat el lite /sat ′ ə līt ′/ *n.* **1.** a heavenly body that moves in an orbit around another body larger than itself. **2.** a spacecraft that moves in an orbit around the earth, the moon, or other bodies in space.

sat is fac tion /sat ′ is fak ′ shən/ *n.* the condition of being satisfied or the act of satisfying.

Sat urn /sat ′ ərn/ *n.* the second largest planet in our solar system. It is the sixth planet in order of distance from the sun. Saturn is surrounded by large rings and many moons.

sau na /sô nə, sou ′ nə/ *n.* **1.** a bath, similar to a steambath, in which the bather is surrounded by hot, dry air. **2.** a room in which to take such a bath.

scent /sent/ *n.* **1.** a smell. **2.** the trail by which someone or something can be traced or found. *—v.* to sense by or as if by the sense of smell. *The dogs scented the rabbit.*

sched ule /skej ′ ül/ *n.* **1.** a list of times, events, or things to do. **2.** the time at which something is sup-posed to happen. *—v.* **sched uled, sched ul ing.** to put in or on a sched-ule; plan or arrange for a particular time.

/a/	at
/ā/	ape
/ä/	far
/â/	care
/e/	end
/ē/	me
/i/	it
/ī/	ice
/î/	pierce
/o/	hot
/ō/	old
/ô/	song
/ôr/	fork
/oi/	oil
/ou/	out
/u/	up
/ū/	use
/ü/	rule
/ù/	pull
/ûr/	turn
/ch/	chin
/ng/	sing
/sh/	shop
/th/	thin
/th/	this
/hw/	white
/zh/	treasure
/ə/	about
	taken
	pencil
	lemon

scheme /skēm/ *n.* **1.** a plan or plot for doing something. **2.** an orderly arrangement of related things; design. —*v.* **schemed, schem ing.** to plan or plot.

schol ar ship /skol ′ ər ship ′/ *n.* **1.** money that is given to a student to help pay for his or her studies. **2.** knowledge or learning.

scis sors /siz ′ ərz/ *pl. n.* a tool used for cutting paper, thread, cardboard, cloth, and many other kinds of material. Scissors have two blades held together in the middle. When the blades are brought together, they form a double cutting edge.

se cu ri ty /si kyùr ′ i tē/ *n., pl.* **se cu ri ties. 1.** protection from harm or loss; safety. **2.** something that gives protection. **3.** something that is given to make sure an agreement will be fulfilled.

sen tence /sen ′ təns/ *n.* a group of words that gives a complete thought. A sentence states something or asks a question. —*v.* **1.** to divide into sections; give out in parts. **2.** a punishment for crime set by a court. —*v.* **sen tenced, sen tenc ing.** to set the punishment of.

ser geant /sär ′ jənt/ *n.* **1.** an army or marine officer who ranks below a lieutenant but above a corporal. **2.** an air force enlisted person who ranks above an airman.

ser vice /sûr ′ vis/ *n.* **1.** a helpful act; useful work. **2.** a system or way of giving something needed or requested by a person or people. **3.** a branch of the armed forces. —*v.* **ser viced, ser vic ing.** to make or keep ready for use.

set tle ment /set ′ əl mənt/ *n.* **1.** the act of settling or the condition of being settled. **2.** a small village or group of houses. *Pioneers built many settlements.*

sher iff /sher ′ if/ *n.* the main officer responsible for enforcing the law in a county. The sheriff is also in charge of taking care of the jails.

shop /shop/ *n.* **1.** a place where goods are sold. **2.** a place where a particular kind of work is done. —*v.* **shopped, shop ping.** to visit stores in order to look at and buy goods.

show er /shou ′ ər/ *n.* **1.** a brief fall of rain. **2.** a fall of anything in larger numbers. **3.** a bath in which water is sprayed on a person from overhead. —*v.* **1.** to fall or make fall in a shower. **2.** to bathe by taking a shower. —**show er y,** *adj.*

shrewd /shrüd/ *adj.* clever and sharp. *The shrewd customer found a bargain.*—**shrewd ly,** *adv.*—**shrewd ness,** *n.*

shrub ber y /shrub ′ ə rē/ *n., pl.* **shrub ber ies. 1.** a group of shrubs. **2.** a plot of ground planted with shrubs.

sig nif i cant /sig nif ′ i kənt/ *adj.* having special value or meaning; important. *July 20, 1969, was a significant date in history because it was the day of the first moon landing.* —**sig nif i cant ly,** *adv.*

slip per y /slip ′ ə rē/ *adj.* **slip per i er, slip per i est. 1.** causing or likely to cause slipping or sliding. **2.** slipping or sliding away easily.
—**slip per i ness,** *n.*

smooth /smü<u>th</u>/ *adj.* **1.** having a surface that is not uneven or rough. **2.** even or gentle in movement. **3.** free from difficulties or trouble. —*v.* **1.** to make even or level or remove what is keeping something from being smooth. **2.** to free from difficulty.

snap shot /snap ′ shot ′/ *n.* an informal photograph that is taken with a small, often inexpensive camera.

snow flake /snō ′ flāk ′/ *n.* one of the small ice crystals that fall as snow.

sol dier /sol ′ jər/ *n.* a person who is a member of an army.

sol emn /sol ′ əm/ *adj.* serious; grave. *They made a solemn promise never to reveal the secret.*

sol i tude /sol ′ i tüd ′, sol ′ i tūd ′/ *n.* **1.** the state of being or living alone; loneliness. **2.** a lonely or unvisited place.

som er sault /sum ′ ər sôlt ′/ *v.* to roll the body by turning the heels over the head. —*n.* a roll of the body done by turning the heels over the head.

sou ve nir /sü ′ və nir′, sü ′ və nîr ′/ *n.* something that is kept because it reminds one of a person, place, or event.

spa ghet ti /spə get ′ ē/ *n.* a food that looks like long, thin strings. It is made of a mixture of flour and water. Spaghetti is a kind of pasta.

spe cif ic /spi sif ′ ik/ *adj.* **1.** exact; particular. *Nine hundred dollars is the specific amount of money you need to buy this used car.* **2.** stated in a way that is easily understood; clear.

spec tac u lar /spek tak ′ yə lər/ *adj.* very unusual or impressive.
—**spec tac u lar ly,** *adv.*

starve /stärv/ *v.* **starved, starv ing. 1.** to suffer from or die of hunger. **2.** to be very hungry.

stead y /sted ′ ē/ *adj.* **stead i er, stead i est. 1.** firm in movement or position; not shaky. **2.** not easily upset; calm. —*v.* **stead ied, stead y ing.** to make or become steady.
—**stead i ly,** *adv.* —**stead i ness,** *n.*

strug gle /strug ′ əl/ *v.* **strug gled, strug gling. 1.** to make a great effort. **2.** to fight; battle. —*n.* **1.** a great effort. **2.** a fight, battle, or war.

stub born /stub ′ ərn/ *adj.* **1.** not yielding. **2.** hard to overcome or deal with. *My stubborn cold lasted a month.*
—**stub born ly,** *adv.*
—**stub born ness,** *n.*

stur dy /stûr ′ dē/ *adj.* **stur di er, stur di est. 1.** strong; hardy. **2.** hard to overcome. —**stur di ly,** *adv.*

sub- a prefix that means **1.** under; below; beneath. **2.** nearly; less than. **3.** used to express a further division or distinction. **4.** lower in position.

/a/	at
/ā/	ape
/ä/	far
/â/	care
/e/	end
/ē/	me
/i/	it
/ī/	ice
/î/	pierce
/o/	hot
/ō/	old
/ô/	song
/ôr/	fork
/oi/	oil
/ou/	out
/u/	up
/ū/	use
/ü/	rule
/ù/	pull
/ûr/	turn
/ch/	chin
/ng/	sing
/sh/	shop
/th/	thin
/<u>th</u>/	this
/hw/	white
/zh/	treasure
/ə/	about
	taken
	pencil
	lemon

sub con scious /sub kon ′ shəs/ *adj.*
1. existing in the mind but only partially perceived by the consciousness. *a subconscious wish.* **2.** not completely conscious. —*n.* the part of the mind that retains experiences and feelings that are difficult to bring back to awareness often because awareness of them would be painful or produce anxiety. —**sub con scious ly,** *adv.* **sub con scious ness,** *n.*

sub due /səb dü ′, səb dū ′/ *v.* **sub dued, sub du ing. 1.** to defeat; conquer. **2.** to control or overcome. *to subdue fear.* —**sub du er,** *n.*

sub ject /sub ′ jikt, səb jekt ′/ *n.* **1.** something thought or talked about. **2.** a course or field that is studied. **3.** a word or group of words in a sentence that tells whom or what the sentence is about. —*adj.* **1.** under the control of a person or organization. **2.** likely to be affected; liable to have. —*v.* **1.** to bring under control. **2.** to cause to experience.

sub mar ine /sub ′ mə rēn ′, sub ′ mə rēn ′/ *n.* **1.** a ship that can travel under water. **2.** a sandwich made with one long loaf of bread. —*adj.* growing or lying underwater.

sub merge /səb mûrj ′/ *v.* **sub merged, sub merg ing. 1.** to cover with a liquid. **2.** to go beneath the surface of water or another liquid. *The diver submerged to look for the sunken ship.* —**sub mer gence,** *n.*

sub scribe /səb skrīb ′/ *v.* **sub scribed, sub scrib ing. 1.** to agree to receive and pay for. **2.** to give or show one's

agreement or approval. —**sub scrib er,** *n.*

sub se quent /sub ′ si kwənt/ *adj.* happening after; coming as a result. *Subsequent experiments showed the same results as the first experiment.* —**sub se quent ly,** *adv.*

sub stance /sub ′ stəns/ *n.* **1.** the material that something is made of. **2.** the important part of something; meaning.

sub sti tute /sub ′ sti tüt ′, sub ′ sti tūt ′/ *n.* a person who does something in place of another; a thing used instead of another. —*v.* **sub sti tut ed, sub sti tut ing. 1.** to put in place of another. **2.** to take the place of another.

sub ter ra ne an /sub ′ tə rā ′ nē ən/ *adj.* being, located, or happening below the surface of the earth; underground.

sub trac tion /səb trak ′ shən/ *n.* the subtracting of one number from another number to find the difference.

sub ur ban /sə bûr ′ bən/ *adj.* of or having to do with a suburb. *My parents commute between the city and our suburban community.*

suc cess /sək ses ′/ *n., pl.* **suc cess es. 1.** a result that has been hoped for; favorable end. **2.** a person or thing that does or goes well.

sug ges tion /səg jes ′ chən, sə jes ′ chən/ *n.* **1.** the act of suggesting something. **2.** something suggested. **3.** a hint; trace.

adj. adjective
adv. adverb
conj. conjunction
contr. contraction
def. definition
interj. interjection
n. noun
pl. plural
prep. preposition
pron. pronoun
sing. singular
v. verb
v.i. intransitive verb
v.t. transitive verb

suit a ble /sü ′ tə bəl/ *adj.* right; proper. *The soil is suitable for growing crops.* —**suit a bil i ty, suit a ble ness,** *n.* —**suit a bly,** *adv.*

super- a prefix that means **1.** over; above. **2.** higher or greater; superior.

su perb /sü pûrb ′/ *adj.* very fine; excellent. *a superb performance.* —**su perb ly,** *adv.*

su per high way /sü ′ pər hī ′ wā/ *n.* a highway designed for high speeds, usually having four or more lanes with a center strip separating traffic going in opposite directions.

su per in tend ent /sü pər in ten ′dənt/ *n.* a person who directs or manages something. *The superintendent of police is the head of the police department.*

su pe ri or /sə pîr ′ ē ər/ *adj.* **1.** higher, greater, or better. **2.** proud; haughty. —*n.* a person who is in a higher position.

su per la tive /sə pûr ′ lə tiv/ *adj.* of the highest sort; above all others —*n.* the form of an adjective or adverb that shows the greatest degree of whatever is expressed by the basic form. *Darkest is the superlative of dark.* —**su per la tive ly,** *adv.* —**su per la tive ness,** *n.*

su per mar ket /sü ′ pər mär ′ kit/ *n.* a large store that sells food and household goods.

su per sede /sü pər sēd ′/ *v.* **su per sed ed, su per sed ing. 1.** to take the place of; replace. **2.** to take the job or office of; succeed. —**su per sed er,** *n.*

su per son ic /sü pər son ′ ik/ *adj.* of, relating to, or traveling at a speed greater than the speed of sound in air, approximately 740 miles (1,190 kilometers) per hour at sea level.

su per sti tion /sü pər stish ′ ən/ *n.* a belief based on ignorance and fear. *The belief that a black cat will bring bad luck is a superstition.*

su per vise /sü ′ pər vīz ′/ *v.* **su per vised, su per vis ing.** to watch over and direct.

su per vi sor /sü ′ pər vī ′ zər/ *n.* a person who watches over and directs the work of other people.

su preme /sə prēm ′/ *adj.* **1.** greatest in power or authority; most important. **2.** highest; utmost. —**su preme ly,** *adv.*

sur ren der /sə ren ′ dər/ *v.* to yield. —*n.* the act of surrendering.

sur vey ing /sər vā ′ ing/ *n.* the act, science, or occupation of making land surveys.

sur vi vor /sər vī ′ vər/ *n.* a person or thing that survives or lives through. *two survivors of the crash.*

sus pense /sə spens ′/ *n.* the condition of being in doubt and worried about what will happen. *The exciting movie kept me in suspense.* —**sus pense ful,** *adj.*

sus pen sion /sə spen ′ shən/ *n.* the act of suspending. *My suspension from school lasted a week.*

/a/	at
/ā/	ape
/ä/	far
/â/	care
/e/	end
/ē/	me
/i/	it
/ī/	ice
/î/	pierce
/o/	hot
/ō/	old
/ô/	song
/ôr/	fork
/oi/	oil
/ou/	out
/u/	up
/ū/	use
/ü/	rule
/u̇/	pull
/ûr/	turn
/ch/	chin
/ng/	sing
/sh/	shop
/th/	thin
/th/	this
/hw/	white
/zh/	treasure
/ə/	about
	taken
	pencil
lemon	

Switz er land /swit ′ sər lənd/ *n.* a country in central Europe.

sword /sôrd/ *n.* a weapon that has a long sharp blade set in a handle. **—sword like,** *adj.*

syl la ble /sil ′ ə bəl/ *n.* **1.** a spoken sound without interruption that forms a word or part of a word. The word *break* has one syllable. The word *important* has three syllables. **2.** a letter or group of letters that form a syllable.

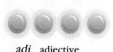

adj. adjective
adv. adverb
conj. conjunction
contr. contraction
def. definition
interj. interjection
n. noun
pl. plural
prep. preposition
pron. pronoun
sing. singular
v. verb
v.i. intransitive verb
v.t. transitive verb

tech nique /tek ′ nēk ′/ *n.* a method or way of bringing about a desired result in science, art, sport, or profession.

ter ri fic /tə rif ′ ik/ *adj.* **1.** unusually great or severe. **2.** causing terror; frightening. **3.** extremely good; wonderful. *That's a terrific idea.*

Thai land /tī ′ land ′/ *n.* a country in southeastern Asia.

thank less /thangk ′ lis/ *adj.* **1.** not likely to be rewarded or appreciated. *a thankless task.* **2.** not feeling gratitude; not grateful. **—thank less ly,** *adv.* **—thank less ness,** *n.*

the a ter /thē ′ ə tər/ *n.* a building or place where plays or motion pictures are presented.

theme /thēm/ *n.* **1.** the main subject or idea of something. **2.** the main melody in a piece of music. **3.** a short piece of writing on one subject; essay.

ther mom e ter /thər mom ′ i tər/ *n.* a device for measuring temperature. Some thermometers are glass tubes containing mercury or alcohol that moves as the temperature changes. Other thermometers show the temperature in other ways.

thick en /thik ′ ən/ *v.* to make or become thick or thicker. **—thick en er,** *n.*

thorn /thôrn/ *n.* **1.** a sharp point on a branch or stem. **2.** a tree or shrub that has thorns.

thor ough /thûr ′ ō/ *adj.* leaving nothing out; careful and complete. **—thor ough ly,** *adv.* **—thor ough ness,** *n.*

thou sand /thou ′ zənd/ *n.* ten times a hundred; 1,000.

throat /thrōt/ *n.* the passage in the body between the mouth and the esophagus.

through /thrü/ *prep.* **1.** from the beginning to the end of. **2.** in one side and out the other side of. **3.** in the midst of. **—adv.** **1.** from one side or end to the other side or end. **2.** completely; totally. **—adj.** **1.** allowing passage from one place to another with no obstruction. **2.** having reached a point of completion; finished.

tol er ant /tol ′ ər ənt/ *adj.* willing to respect or try to understand customs, ideas, or beliefs that are different from one's own. **—tol er ant ly,** *adv.*

to ma to /tə mā ′ tō, tə mä ′ tō/ *n., pl.* **to ma toes.** the round juicy fruit of a plant. The fruit is usually red when ripe and is eaten either raw or cooked.

tongue /tung/ *n.* **1.** a movable piece of flesh in the mouth. It is used for tasting and swallowing. **2.** a language. *Spanish is her native tongue.*

tor ment /tôr ment ′/ *v.* to cause someone great pain or suffering. /tôr ′ ment/ —*n.* great pain or suffering.

tour ist /tùr ′ ist/ *n.* a person who is traveling for pleasure or to learn about other places.

tra di tion /trə dish ′ ən/ *n.* **1.** the practice of passing down customs, beliefs, or other knowledge from parents to their children. **2.** a custom or belief that is passed on in this way.

trai tor /trā ′ tər/ *n.* a person who does something to harm his or her own country or friends; one who betrays a group or cause. *The traitors gave secrets to the enemy.*

trans por ta tion /trans ′ pər tā ′ shən/ *n.* the act or means of carrying or moving something from one place to another.

trap e zoid /trap ′ ə zoid ′/ *n.* a figure having four sides with only two sides parallel.

trav el /trav ′ əl/ *v.* to go from one place to another; make a trip.

trav e logue /trav ′ ə lôg ′, trav ′ ə log/ *n.* **1.** a lecture describing a trip, as to a foreign country, often illustrated with slides or films. **2.** a motion picture about a particular country or region.

treach er ous /trech ′ ər əs/ *adj.* **1.** betraying one's country or friends; disloyal. **2.** full of danger; hazardous. —**treach er ous ly,** *adv.* —**treach er ous ness,** *n.*

tre men dous /tri men ′ dəs/ *adj.* very large or great; enormous.

tri- a prefix that means having or involving three.

tri an gle /trī ′ ang ′ gəl/ *n.* a figure or object with three sides and three angles.

tri an gu lar /trī ang ′ gyə lər/ *adj.* having to do with or like a triangle. *The tent had a triangular shape.*

tri cy cle /trī ′ si kəl/ *n.* a vehicle with two wheels in the back and one in front. It is moved by pedaling and steered with handlebars.

tri plets /trip ′ lits/ *n. pl.* of **triplet.** one of three children or animals born at the same time to the same mother.

trip li cate /trip ′ li kit, trip ′ li kāt ′/ *adj.* three times as much or as many; triple. —*n.* one of three identical things, especially copies of printed matter. —*v.* **trip li cat ed, trip li cat ing.** to multiply by three; triple. —**trip li ca tion,** *n.*

tri pod /trī ′ pod/ *n.* a stand with three legs used to hold up a telescope or some other instrument.

adj. adjective
adv. adverb
conj. conjunction
contr. contraction
def. definition
interj. interjection
n. noun
pl. plural
prep. preposition
pron. pronoun
sing. singular
v. verb
v.i. intransitive verb
v.t. transitive verb

un- a prefix that means the opposite of; not.

un beat en /un bē ′ tən/ *adj.* **1.** never defeated or surpassed. **2.** not walked over. *an unbeaten path.*

un friend ly /un frend ′ lē/ *adj.* **un friend li er, un friend li est. 1.** feeling or showing dislike; not friendly. **2.** not pleasant or favorable. *The Arctic is known for its cold, unfriendly climate.* —**un friend li ness,** *n.*

uni- a prefix that means only one; single.

u ni corn /ū ′ ni kôrn ′/ *n.* an imaginary animal that looks like a white horse with a long pointed horn in the middle of its forehead.

u ni cy cle /ū ′ nə sī ′ kəl/ *n.* a vehicle that has pedals and a seat like a bicycle but has only one wheel and no handlebars. It is used mostly by acrobats and other entertainers.

u ni form /ū ′ nə fôrm/ *adj.* **1.** always the same; not changing. **2.** showing little or no difference; all alike. —*n.* the special or official clothes that the members of a particular group wear. —**u ni form ly,** *adv.* —**u ni form ness,** *n.*

un ion /ūn ′ yən/ *n.* **1.** a joining together of two or more people or things. **2.** something formed by a joining together; confederation.

u nique /ū nēk ′/ *adj.* not having an equal; being the only one of its kind. —**u nique ly,** *adv.* —**u nique ness,** *n.*

u ni son /ū ′ nə sən, ū ′ nə zən/ *n.* making the same sounds or movements at the same time. *The students recited the poem in unison.*

u nite /ū nīt ′/ *v.* **u nit ed, u nit ing.** to bring or join together; make or become one. *The two families were united by marriage.*

u ni ty /ū ′ ni tē/ *n., pl.* **u ni ties. 1.** the condition of being one. **2.** the condition of harmony. *The goal of the United Nations is unity in the world.*

u ni verse /ū ′ nə vûrs ′/ *n.* everything that exists, including the earth, the planets, the stars, and all of space.

un paid /un pād/ *adj.* **1.** not yet paid. **2.** serving without pay; unsalaried. *an unpaid volunteer.*

un ru ly /un rü ′ lē/ *adj.* **un ru li er, un ru li est.** hard to control or manage. *an unruly mob.* —**un ru li ness,** *n.*

un self ish /un sel ′ fish/ *adj.* not selfish; generous. —**un self ish ly,** adv. —**un self ish ness,** *n.*

un u su al /un ū ′ zhü əl/ *adj.* not usual, common, or ordinary; rare. —**un u su al ly,** *adv.* —**un u su al ness,** *n.*

U ra nus /yùr ′ ə nəs, yù rā ′ nəs/ *n.* the third largest planet in our solar system. It is the seventh planet in distance from the sun. Uranus is surrounded by rings.

U ru guay /yùr ′ ə gwā ′, ùr ′ ə gwī ′/ *n.* a country in southeastern South America.

use less /ūs ′ lis/ *adj.* **1.** serving no purpose; having no use. **2.** not bring-ing about any result; vain; futile. *It is useless to struggle against such odds.* **—use less ly,** *adv.* **—use less ness,** *n.*

va cate /vā ′ kāt/ *v.* **va cat ed, va cat ing.** to cease to occupy; leave empty. *The tenant decided to vacate the apartment.*

va ca tion /vā kā ′ shən/ *n.* a period of rest or freedom from school, busi-ness, or other activity. **—v.** to take or spend a vacation. **—va ca tion er,** *n.*

vag a bond /vag ′ ə bond ′/ *n.* a per-son who wanders from place to place, having no regular home.

val u able /val ′ ū ə bəl, val ′ yə bəl/ *adj.* **1.** worth much money. **2.** having great use or importance. *My summer job was a valuable experience for me.*

va nil la /və nil ′ ə/ *n.* a flavoring that is used in candies, ice cream, cookies, and other foods. Vanilla comes from the seed pods of a tropical plant that is a type of orchid.

vault /vôlt/ *n.* **1.** an arched structure serving as a roof or ceiling. **2.** a safe room or compartment that is used to store money or other things of value.

veg e ta tion /vej ′ i tā ′ shən/ *n.* plant life.

ve loc i ty /və los ′ i tē/ *n., pl.* **ve loc i ties.** the rate of motion; speed. *The baseball was pitched at a velocity close to 95 miles per hour.*

Ven e zue la /ven ′ ə zwā ′ lə, ven ′ ə zwē ′ lə/ *n.* a country in northern South America. **—Ven e zue lan,** *adj., n.*

ven om ous /ven ′ ə məs/ *adj.* **1.** able to inflict a poisonous wound, espe-cially by biting or stinging. *a ven-omous snake.* **2.** containing or full of venom. **3.** malicious, spiteful. *a ven-omous remark.* **—ven om ous ly,** *adv.* **—ven om ous ness,** *n.*

Ve nus /vē ′ nəs/ *n.* the sixth largest planet in our solar system. It is the second planet in order of distance from the sun and the one nearest earth.

vi cious /vish ′ əs/ *adj.* **1.** wicked, evil. **2.** full of spite; malicious. *vicious lies.* **3.** fierce or dangerous. *the vicious dog.* **—vi cious ly,** *adv.* **—vi cious ness,** *n.*

Vi et nam /vē ′ et näm ′/ *n.* a country in southeastern Asia.

vig or ous /vig ′ ər əs/ *adj.* full of or done with vigor. *Our dog is still just as vigorous as it was when it was a puppy.* **—vig or ous ly,** *adv.*

vi o lence /vī ′ ə ləns/ *n.* **1.** strong physical force used to harm. **2.** great or destructive force or action. *The violence of the hurricane left few houses standing.*

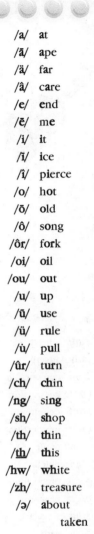

/a/	at
/ā/	ape
/ä/	far
/â/	care
/e/	end
/ē/	me
/i/	it
/ī/	ice
/î/	pierce
/o/	hot
/ō/	old
/ô/	song
/ôr/	fork
/oi/	oil
/ou/	out
/u/	up
/ū/	use
/ü/	rule
/ù/	pull
/ûr/	turn
/ch/	chin
/ng/	sing
/sh/	shop
/th/	thin
/<u>th</u>/	this
/hw/	white
/zh/	treasure
/ə/	about
	taken
	pencil

lemon

vow el /vou ′ əl/ *n.* **1.** a speech sound made by not blocking the flow of air through the mouth. **2.** a letter that represents such a sound. *A, e, i, o, u,* and sometimes *y* are vowels.

Voy ag er /voi ′ i jər/ *n.* the name of a spaceship.

waltz /wôlts/ *n., pl.* **waltz es. 1.** a whirling, gliding dance that is performed by a couple. **2.** the music for this dance. —*v.* to dance a waltz. —**waltz er,** *n.*

wea ver /wē ′ vər/ *n.* a person who weaves or whose work is weaving.

weight less /wāt ′ lis/ *adj.* **1.** having little or no weight. **2.** not influenced by the pull of gravity. —**weight less ness,** *n.*

weird /wîrd/ *adj.* strange or mysterious; odd. —**weird ly,** *adv.* —**weird ness,** *n.*

wharf /hwôrf, wôrf/ *n., pl.* **wharves** or **wharfs.** a structure built along a shore as a landing place for boats and ships; dock.

wheel bar row /hwēl ′ bar ′ ō, wēl ′ bar ′ ō/ *n.* a small cart with one or two wheels at the front end and two handles at the back for pushing.

wheth er /hwe<u>th</u> ′ ər, we<u>th</u> ′ ər/ *conj.* **1.** a word that is used to introduce a choice between things. **2.** if. *Let me*

know whether you can come to my party.

whirl wind /whûrl ′ wind ′, wûrl ′ wind ′/ *n.* a rapidly or violently rotating column of air.

whis tle /hwis ′ əl, wis ′ əl/ *v.* **whis tled, whis tling. 1.** to make a clear, sharp sound by forcing air out through rounded lips or through the teeth. **2.** to make or move with a sound like this. —*n.* a device that makes a clear, sharp sound when air is blown through it. —**whist ler,** *n.*

whit tle /hwit ′ əl, wit ′ əl/ *v.* **whit tled, whit tling.** to make or shape by cutting away small bits with a knife. —**whit tler,** *n.*

whole some /hōl ′ səm/ *adj.* good for the health. —**whole some ness,** *n.*

whol ly /hō ′ lē, hōl ′ lē/ *adv.* to the whole amount or extent; entirely; completely.

whom /hüm/ *pron.* what or which person or persons. *I don't know whom I liked best in the play.*

with stand /with stand ′, wi<u>th</u> stand ′/ *v.* **with stood, with stand ing.** to resist the effects of; hold out against. *The little boat withstood the storm and reached the shore safely.*

won der ful /wun ′ dər fəl/ *adj.* **1.** causing wonder; remarkable. **2.** very good; fine. —**won der ful ly,** *adv.* —**won der ful ness,** *n.*

world /wûrld/ *n.* **1.** the earth. **2.** a part of the earth. **3.** all the people who live on the earth.

adj.	adjective
adv.	adverb
conj.	conjunction
contr.	contraction
def.	definition
interj.	interjection
n.	noun
pl.	plural
prep.	preposition
pron.	pronoun
sing.	singular
v.	verb
v.i.	intransitive verb
v.t.	transitive verb

...Y.............

-y a suffix used to form adjectives or nouns. The adjective form means characterized by; the noun form means state or quality.

yacht /yot/ *n.* a small ship used for pleasure trips.

yawn /yôn/ *v.* to open the mouth wide and take a deep breath. —*n.* the act of opening the mouth wide and taking a deep breath.

yo gurt /yō ′ gərt/ *n.* a thick soft food that is made by adding certain bacteria to milk. Yogurt is often sweetened and flavored with fruit.

you're /yùr, yôr; *unstressed* yər/ *contr.* shortened form of "you are."

youth /ūth/ *n.* **1.** the condition or quality of being young. **2.** the time of life after childhood and before becoming an adult.

/a/	at
/ā/	ape
/ä/	far
/â/	care
/e/	end
/ē/	me
/i/	it
/ī/	ice
/î/	pierce
/o/	hot
/ō/	old
/ô/	song
/ôr/	fork
/oi/	oil
/ou/	out
/u/	up
/ū/	use
/ü/	rule
/ù/	pull
/ûr/	turn
/ch/	chin
/ng/	sing
/sh/	shop
/th/	thin
/th/	this
/hw/	white
/zh/	treasure
/ə/	about
	taken
	pencil
	lemon

...Z.............

Zam bi a /zam ′ bē ə/ *n.* a country in central Africa.

zuc chi ni /zü kē ′ nē/ *n., pl,*
zuc chi ni or **zuc chi nis.** a green summer squash shaped like a cucumber, eaten as a vegetable.

LESSON 1

Focus
page 2

1–15. unselfish, possible, accent, messenger, publish, snapshot, withstand, athletic, rapid, significant, mathematics, dismiss, penniless, establish, suspense

16–20. velocity, optimum, discipline, recommend, necessity

Words and Meanings
page 3
1. athletic
2. significant
3. withstand
4. possible
5. establish
6. penniless
7. messenger
8. suspense
9. dismiss
10. rapid
11. publish
12. snapshot
13. accent
14. mathematics
15. unselfish

Word Works
16. unathletic (not athletic)
17. uncomfortable (not comfortable)
18. unequal (not equal)
19. unhealthy (not healthy)
20. unimportant (not important)

Word Play
page 4
1–9. mathematics, establish, messenger, suspense, publish, possible, athletic, significant, rapid
10. snapshot
11. dismiss
12. unselfish
13. penniless
14. accent
15. withstand

Write on Your Own
page 5
Lists will vary. Students should use four Core Words. The Write on Your Own activities need not always result in finished or published writing. Often it is more productive to focus on a particular aspect of good writing and allow students to experiment with various revisions without evaluation.

Proofreading Practice
1–5. rapid, significant, athletic, possible, snapshot

LESSON 2

Focus
page 6

1–15. reply, snowflake, breathe, equator, reminder, theme, vacate, devote, maintain, realize, rodeo, traitor, receive, migrate, release

16–20. microphone, wheelbarrow, supervisor, peculiar, receipt

Words and Meanings
page 7
1. release
2. vacate
3. equator
4. breathe
5. devote
6. snowflake
7. migrate
8. rodeo
9. maintain
10. traitor
11. realize
12. reply
13. reminder
14. theme
15. receive

Word Works
16. devotion
17. vacation
18. migration
19. creation
20. donation

Word Play
page 8
1. migrate
2. theme
3. maintain
4. traitor
5. devote
6. rodeo
7. equator
8. breathe
9. realize
10. release
11. receive
12. reply ,
13. reminder
14. snowflake
15. vacate

Write on Your Own
page 9
Letters will vary. Students should use four Core Words. Check to see that students use exact words to describe how they felt and what they saw.

Proofreading Practice
1–5. receive, breathe, devote, maintain, rodeo

LESSON 3

Focus
page 10

1–2. waltz, almanac
3–5. awning, yawned, awkward
6–15. faulty, haughty, launch, fraud, applaud, vault, haunch, author, daughter, laundry
16–20. somersault, laundromat, sauna, auditorium, inaugurate

Words and Meanings
page 11
1. author
2. daughter
3. launch
4. haunch
5. awkward
6. laundry
7. waltz
8. applaud
9. faulty
10. awning
11. vault
12. haughty
13. fraud
14. yawned
15. almanac

Word Works
16. haughtiest
17. naughtier
18. worthiest
19. dirtier
20. juiciest

Word Play
page 12
1. Waltz
2. Applaud
3. Author
4. Almanac
5. Fraud
6. Awkward
7. vault
8. daughter
9–10. launch, haunch
11–12. awning, yawned
13–15. faulty, haughty, laundry
16–20. almanac, applaud, author, awkward, awning

Write on Your Own
page 13
Diary entries will vary. Students should use four Core Words. Check to see that students use the first person, or "I/me" point of view.

Proofreading Practice
1–4. waltz, daughter, haughty, awkward

LESSON 4

Focus
page 14

1–15. dd: pudding; ll: vanilla, alligator, bulletin, gorilla, alley; mm: commercial, hammock, commuter; nn: annual, antenna, innocent, channel; rr: hurricane; ss: dissolve
16–20. parallel, immediate, corridor, exaggerate, immense

Words and Meanings
page 15
1. annual
2. hammock
3. vanilla
4. pudding
5. channel
6. bulletin
7. commercial
8. dissolve
9. antenna
10. hurricane
11. commuter
12. alley
13. alligator
14. gorilla
15. innocent

Word Works
Answers may vary.
16. guilty
17. forget
18. apart
19. funny
20. real

Word Play
page 16
1–4. commuter, commercial, alley, alligator
5. innocent
6. pudding
7. dissolve
8. bulletin
9. gorilla
10. annual
11. antenna
12. bulletin
13. hurricane
14. hammock
15. vanilla

Write on Your Own
page 17
Bulletins will vary. Students should use four Core Words. Check to see that students were able to write concise, meaningful bulletins.

Proofreading Practice
1–4. commercial, gorilla, antenna, vanilla
5. Karrie
6. She
7. antenna.

LESSON 5

Focus
page 18

1–10. census, niece, certificate, service, celebrate, sacrifice, fierce, crevice, presence, century

11–15. specific, circuit, circular, cylinder, civil

16–19. (ci)tation, (ce)metery, (ce)ramic, (ci)rcumstan(ce)

20. scent

Words and Meanings
page 19

1. fierce
2. civil
3. certificate
4. sacrifice
5. circuit
6. crevice
7. census
8. presence
9. service
10. cylinder
11. specific
12. circular
13. century
14. celebrate
15. niece

Word Works

16. circle
17. circus
18. circuit

Word Play
page 20

1. census
2. presence
3. cylinder
4. century
5. fierce
6. service
7. niece
8. celebrate
9. civil
10–15. specific, certificate, circuit, sacrifice, circular, crevice
16. niece
17. cylinder
18. sacrifice
19. circuit
20. specific

Write on Your Own
page 21

Ads will vary. Students should use four Core Words. Check to see that students used concrete details.

Proofreading Practice

1–5. specific, fierce, service, sacrifice, circular

REVIEW LESSON 6

1. mathematics
2. snapshot
3. publish
4. athletic
5. reply
6. theme
7. migrate
8. reminder
9. vault
10. applaud
11. fraud
12. almanac
13. innocent
14. annual
15. commuter
16. hurricane
17. fierce
18. niece
19. century
20. sacrifice

LESSON 7

Focus
page 24

1–5. chocolate, chimney, cheddar, chamber, charcoal

6–8. abolish, astonish, rubbish

9–12. thicken, whether, thorn, theater

13-16. whether, whirlwind, overwhelm, whittle

17-21. (sh)rubbery, (ch)ieftain, (wh)arf, (th)ermometer, my(th)ology

Words and Meanings
page 25

1. thicken
2. chamber
3. chimney
4. rubbish
5. charcoal
6. cheddar
7. chocolate
8. whirlwind
9. whether
10. thorn
11. overwhelm
12. abolish
13. astonish
14. theater
15. whittle

Word Works

16. weather
17. steel
18. which
19. board
20. cereal

Word Play
page 26

1. thorn
2. abolish
3. thicken
4. astonish
5. chocolate
6–8. cheddar, rubbish, whittle
9. chimney
10–11. overwhelm, charcoal
12. whirlwind
13–15. whether, chamber, theater
16. as/ton/ish
17. choc/o/late
18. thick/en
19. a/bol/ish
20. the/a/ter

Write on Your Own
page 27

Notes will vary. Students should use four Core Words. For a peer evaluation, have students compare their notes in pairs and then as a class.

Proofreading Practice

1–4. whether, rubbish, whittle, astonish
5. If
6. you.
7. carving.

LESSON 8

Focus
page 28

1–8. disc(ar)d, b(ar)ge, guit(ar), h(ar)ness, dep(ar)ture, c(ar)bon, p(ar)tially, p(ar)don

9–15. (or)igin, f(or)mula, (or)nament, f(or)tress, (or)ganize, f(or)tunate, (or)dinary

16–20. q(uar)antine, t(or)ment, f(or)mation, ass(or)tment, c(or)dial

Words and Meanings
page 29

1. organize
2. discard
3. formula
4. guitar
5. carbon
6. fortunate
7. harness
8. pardon
9. ordinary
10. fortress
11. barge
12. partially
13. ornament
14. departure
15. origin

Word Works

16. carbonate
17. originate
18. formulate

Word Play
page 30

1. carbon
2. ordinary
3. pardon
4. guitar
5. organize
6. barge
7–8. origin, original; ornament, ornamental
9–10. departure, fortunate
11. partially
12. fortress
13. harness
14. discard
15. formula

Write on Your Own
page 31

Descriptions will vary. Students should use four Core Words. Check to see that students have presented their plans in a logical order.

Proofreading Practice

1–4. ordinary, organize, departure, formula

LESSON 9

Focus
page 32
1–15. yogurt, calendar, desperate, surrender, accurate, surveying, capture, popular, barrier, familiar, emperor, alternate, pressure, admiral, memory
16–20. survivor, burglar, perpetual, calculator, monitor

Words and Meanings
page 33
1. emperor
2. calendar
3. desperate
4. admiral
5. capture
6. barrier
7. surrender
8. pressure
9. surveying
10. alternate
11. memory
12. popular
13. yogurt
14. familiar
15. accurate

Word Works
16. waffle
17. spaghetti
18. hamburger

Word Play
page 34
1. Memory
2. Surrender
3. Barrier
4. Capture
5. Admiral
6. Emperor
7. surveying
8. pressure
9. yogurt
10. alternate
11–12. popular, familiar
13. calendar
14–15. desperate, accurate
16–20. Answers will vary.

Write on Your Own
page 35
Ads will vary. Students should use four Core Words. Look especially for the use of sensory words, words that describe how yogurt smells or tastes, for example.

Proofreading Practice
1–4. alternate, popular, accurate, capture

LESSON 10

Focus***
page 36
1–13. unruly, lagoon, duplicate, numerous, solitude, caboose, group, nuisance, routine, suitable, jewelry, improve, consume
14–15. youth, union
16–20. souvenir, crusader, neutral, illuminate, shrewd

Words and Meanings
page 37
1. numerous
2. group
3. lagoon
4. unruly
5. consume
6. jewelry
7. caboose
8. solitude
9. union
10. youth
11. routine
12. duplicate
13. suitable
14. nuisance
15. improve

Word Works
16. ailment
17. pavement
18. amendment
19. enjoyment
20. statement

Word Play
page 38
1. Duplicate
2. Consume
3. Solitude
4. Union
5. Lagoon
6. caboose
7. youth
8. group
9. jewelry
10. routine
11. improve
12. unruly
13. numerous
14. nuisance
15. suitable

Write on Your Own
page 39
Journal entries will vary. Students should use four Core Words. Students should use interesting and unusual detail.

Proofreading Practice
1–5. lagoon, numerous, unruly, duplicate, improve

LESSON 11

Focus
page 40
Circled and underlined elements may vary.
1–15. adjective, adverb, article, comma, conjunction, consonant, contraction, English, essay, hyphen, predicate, preposition, pronoun, syllable, vowel
16–20. participle, infinitive, phrase, interjection, punctuation

Words and Meanings
page 41
1. article/essay
2. essay/article
3. English
4. comma
5. syllable
6. hyphen
7. contraction
8. vowel/consonant
9. consonant/vowel
10. predicate
11. conjunction
12. adjective
13. adverb
14. pronoun
15. preposition

Word Works
16. essays
17. colonies
18. monkeys
19. decoys
20. rallies

Word Play
page 42
1. adjective
2. contraction
3. conjunction
4. preposition
5. pronoun
6. adverb
7. article
8. consonant
9. vowel
10. syllable
11. comma
12. hyphen
13. predicate
14. English
15. essay/article
16. a composition written for a newspaper, magazine, or book
17. a shortened form
18. the act of joining together or the state of being joined together

Write on Your Own
page 43
Lists will vary. Students should use four Core Words. For assessment, have students develop a group list of rules.

Proofreading Practice
1–4. consonant, pronoun, adjective, English

REVIEW LESSON 12

1. rubbish
2. thorn
3. chimney
4. theater
5. ordinary
6. fortunate
7. pardon
8. guitar
9. surrender
10. accurate
11. familiar
12. capture
13. lagoon
14. caboose
15. group
16. youth
17. contraction
18. article
19. pronoun
20. preposition

LESSON 13

Focus
page 46
1–10. *kn:* knead, knelt, knuckle; *gu:* guest, guardian; *wh:* wholly, wholesome, whom; *kh:* khaki; *gn:* gnash
11–15. sa(l)mon, (h)onesty, (h)erb, solem(n), hus(t)le
16–20. Circled elements may vary. guarantee, rhinoceros, knowledge, spaghetti, rhinestone

Words and Meanings
page 47
1. wholesome
2. salmon
3. herb
4. knead
5. knuckle
6. khaki
7. wholly
8. hustle
9. honesty
10. gnash
11. whom
12. solemn
13. guardian
14. knelt
15. guest

Word Works
16. oxen
17. scissors
18. children
19. feet
20. cacti (or cactuses or cactus)

Word Play
page 48
1. knead
2. wholly
3. guest
4. wholesome
5. Herb
6. khaki
7. solemn
8. gnash
9. guardian
10. honesty
11. knuckle
12. hustle
13. salmon
14. whom
15. knelt

Write on Your Own
page 49
Descriptions will vary. Students should use four Core Words. Check student descriptions for the effective use of sensory words.

Proofreading Practice
1–5. wholesome, khaki, guest, solemn, wholly

LESSON 14

Focus
page 50
Circled elements in items 10–15 may vary.
1–4. dangerous, mountainous, vigorous, humorous
5–9. famous, ridiculous, adventurous, continuous, nervous
10–15. tre(men)d(ous), jeal(ous), (court)e(ous), (pre)vi(ous), (dis)(astr)(ous), vici(ous)
16–20. treacher(ous), boister(ous), venom(ous), ambiti(ous), mischiev(ous)

Words and Meanings
page 51
1. famous
2. disastrous
3. vigorous
4. continuous
5. courteous
6. jealous
7. tremendous
8. dangerous/ vicious
9. vicious/ dangerous
10. adventurous
11. mountainous
12. nervous
13. previous
14. ridiculous
15. humorous

Word Works
16. jealousy
17. fame
18. courtesy
19. disaster
20. viciousness

Word Play
page 52
1. Mountainous
2. Famous
3. Continuous
4. Dangerous
5. Courteous
6. ridiculous
7. disastrous
8. adventurous
9–10. vigorous, humorous
11–15. tremendous, nervous, vicious, jealous, previous

Write on Your Own
page 53
Story openings will vary. Students should use four Core Words. This is a good opportunity to check for good beginnings and endings.

Proofreading Practice
1–4. previous, disastrous, continuous, tremendous

LESSON 15

Focus***
page 54
1–3. bouquet, technique, mosquito
4–16. scheme, chaos, character, headache, schedule, technique, chemistry, mechanic, orchestra, chlorine, chrome, monarchy, chorus
17–21. (ch)romosome, zu(cch)ini, (ch)rysanthemum, s(ch)olarship, (ch)ronological

Words and Meanings
page 55
1. technique
2. chrome
3. mechanic
4. chlorine
5. chemistry
6. chaos
7. character
8. scheme
9. schedule
10. headache
11. orchestra
12. chorus
13. monarchy
14. bouquet
15. mosquito

Word Works
16. mosquitoes
17. echoes
18. zeros
19. heroes
20. radios
21. pianos
22. tomatoes

Word Play
page 56
1–4. chemistry, mosquito, character, monarchy
5. mechanic
6. orchestra
7. chorus
8. chlorine
9. chaos
10. chrome
11. scheme
12. schedule
13–14. bouquet, technique
15. headache
16. noun, verb
17. noun, verb
18. noun, verb

Write on Your Own
page 57
Lists will vary. Students should use four Core Words. Check lists for creative thought processes.

Proofreading Practice
1–5. monarchy, chemistry, chorus, mechanic, mosquito
6. Mars.

LESSON 16

Focus
page 58
1–15. *il-:* (il)legible, (il)legal, (il)literate, (il)logical; *im-:* (im)possible, (im)partial, (im)patient; *in-:* (in)secure, (in)dependent, (in)correct; *ir-:* (ir)rational, (ir)regular; *non-:* (non)violent, (non)profit, (non)standard
16–20. (ir)responsible, (in)conclusive, (in)escapable, (im)personal, (in)capable

Words and Meanings
page 59
1. independent
2. impartial
3. nonprofit
4. insecure
5. impatient
6. illegal
7. irregular/ nonstandard
8. nonstandard/ irregular
9. illiterate
10. incorrect
11. illogical/ irrational
12. irrational/ illogical
13. illegible
14. nonviolent
15. impossible

Word Works
16. impatience
17. nonviolence
18. independence
19. incidence
20. convenience

Word Play
page 60
1. impartial
2. incorrect
3. illegal
4. illegible
5. irrational
6. impatient
7. illogical
8. independent
9. nonviolent
10. nonstandard
11. nonprofit
12. impossible
13. irregular
14. illiterate
15. insecure

Write on Your Own
page 61
Paragraphs will vary. Students should use four Core Words. Review students' writing to see if they have included specific points of comparison.

Proofreading Practice
1–5. independent, illogical, nonviolent, irregular, impatient

LESSON 17

Focus
page 62

You may wish to tell students not to circle letters that spell the schwa sound.

1–9. (U)ranus, Earth, Mars, V(e)nus, Mercur(y), Pl(u)t(o), Saturn, Nept(u)n(e), J(u)piter

10–12. astronaut, asteroid, astronomer

13–15. r(e)entr(y), (e)clipse, satell(i)t(e)

16–20. weightle(ss)ne(ss), Voyager, conste(ll)ation, prope(ll)ant, atmosphere

Words and Meanings
page 63

1. astronomer
2. asteroid
3. eclipse
4. Mercury
5. Venus
6. Earth
7. Mars
8. astronaut
9. reentry
10. Jupiter
11. Saturn
12. satellite
13. Uranus
14. Neptune
15. Pluto

Word Works
16. asteroid: a small rocky body that orbits the sun

17. astronaut: a person who flies in a spacecraft

18. astronomy: the science that deals with heavenly bodies

Word Play
page 64

1. Neptune
2. astronomer
3. Earth
4. astronaut
5. Mercury
6. eclipse
7. satellite
8. Saturn
9. Mars
10. Jupiter
11. reentry
12. Pluto
13. asteroid
14. Venus
15. Uranus

16–20. asteroid, astronaut, astronomer, satellite, Saturn

Write on Your Own
page 65

Poems will vary. Students should use four Core Words. For peer assessment, read or have students read their poems aloud. Comment on sound and rhythm patterns in the poetry.

Proofreading Practice

1–4. Venus, satellite, Pluto, astronaut

REVIEW LESSON 18

1. herb
2. knead
3. knuckle
4. salmon
5. courteous
6. humorous
7. nervous
8. famous
9. character
10. technique
11. scheme
12. chorus
13. illegible
14. incorrect
15. impartial
16. nonprofit
17. eclipse
18. Earth
19. satellite
20. astronomer

LESSON 19

Focus
page 68

1–6. popularity, nationality, humanity, majority, humidity, equality

7–15. unity, ability, security, fiery, hostility, eternity, maturity, injury, slippery

16–20. probabil(ity), econom(y), formal(ity), opportun(ity), neutral(ity)

Words and Meanings
page 69

1. popularity
2. ability
3. fiery
4. equality
5. humidity
6. nationality
7. eternity
8. unity
9. injury
10. security
11. slippery
12. humanity
13. majority
14. hostility
15. maturity

Word Works
16. reprint: to print again
17. recycle: to put through a cycle again
18. relocate: to locate again
19. reassure: to assure again
20. refinish: to finish again

Word Play
page 70

1. ability
2. slippery
3. fiery
4. equality
5. hostility
6. injury
7. maturity
8. eternity
9. security
10–12. unity, humanity, humidity
13. majority
14–15. popularity, nationality

Write on Your Own
page 71

Speeches will vary. Students should use four Core Words. Check to see that students have a logical reason for their positions.

Proofreading Practice

1–4. equality, injury, fiery, ability

LESSON 20

Focus
page 72

1–12. refreshment, kindness, development, amusement, agreement, measurement, cleverness, enchantment, equipment, foolishness, management, settlement

13–15. cleanliness, judgment, loneliness

16–20. astonish(ment), encourage(ment), accomplish(ment), cautious(ness), achieve(ment)

Words and Meanings
page 73

1. amusement
2. development
3. equipment
4. management
5. judgment
6. cleanliness
7. enchantment
8. refreshment
9. loneliness
10. settlement
11. cleverness
12. foolishness
13. measurement
14. agreement
15. kindness

Word Works
16. fieriness
17. loveliness
18. sloppiness
19. cloudiness
20. liveliness
21. greediness
22. clumsiness

Word Play
page 74

1–6. cleverness, development, amusement, kindness, agreement, management
7. settlement
8. equipment
9. cleanliness
10. loneliness
11. enchantment
12. refreshment
13. foolishness
14. measurement
15. judgment
16. fun
17. the act of
18. the quality, state, or condition of being
19. able to be
20. a person who does or makes something

Write on Your Own
page 75

Descriptions will vary. Students should use four Core Words. This writing topic allows an opportunity to check for the use of interesting detail.

Proofreading Practice

1–4. amusement, cleanliness, equipment, enchantment

LESSON 21

Focus
page 76
1–12. integrate, influence, inflate, instinct, inhale, inspire, include, instruct, intrude, increase, involve, ingredient
13–15. im(m)erse, im(p)ose, im(p)ort
16–20. investigate, (indebted), institution, invasion, inhibit

Words and Meanings
page 77
1. influence
2. import
3. impose
4. include
5. inhale
6. instruct
7. instinct
8. intrude/impose
9. inflate
10. increase
11. ingredient
12. immerse
13. involve
14. integrate
15. inspire

Word Works
16. inaccurate
17. immovable
18. invisible
19. impractical
20. indirect

Word Play
page 78
1. instruct
2. include
3. intrude
4. involve
5. impose
6. inspire
7. ingredient
8. instinct
9. influence
10. immerse
11–13. integrate, inflate, inhale
14–15. import, increase
16. in/spire
17. in/spi/ra/tion
18. in/gre/di/ent
19. in/te/grate
20. in/te/gra/tion

Write on Your Own
page 79
Descriptions will vary. Students should use four Core Words. Check to see that students include some precise descriptions of the person such as what he or she said or did.

Proofreading Practice
1–4. influence, integrate, increase, inspire
5–6. King, Jr.,
7. inspire me.

LESSON 22

Focus
page 80
Circled elements may vary.
1–11. remainder, dividend, metric, addition, difference, subtraction, fraction, rectangle, division, calculate, quo(ti)ent
12–15. geometry, perimeter, numerator, multiplication
16–20. trapezoid, denominator, rhombus, circumference, algebra

Words and Meanings
page 81
1. addition
2. multiplication
3. difference
4. subtraction
5. division
6. quotient
7. remainder
8. calculate
9. dividend
10. fraction
11. numerator
12. geometry
13. rectangle
14. perimeter
15. metric

Word Works
16. fragile
17. refraction
18. fraction
19. fracture
20. fragment

Word Play
page 82
1–4. multiplication, addition, division, subtraction
5. quotient
6. dividend
7. remainder
8. difference
9–11. remainder, perimeter, numerator
12. geometry
13. rectangle
14. calculate
15. metric
16. fraction

Write on Your Own
page 83
Paragraphs will vary. Students should use four Core Words. You might have students who like math exchange papers with students who do not like math and evaluate each other's reasons.

Proofreading Practice
1–4. difference, addition, multiplication, calculate

LESSON 23

Focus
page 84
Circled elements may vary.
1–15. Argentina, Bel(gi)um, Botswana, Brazil, Canada, Germany, Great Brit(ai)n, Ireland, Isr(ae)l, Mexico, Pakistan, Swi(tz)erland, (Th)ailand, Vietnam, Zambia
16–20. Ecuador, Egypt, Philippines, Uruguay, Venezuela

Words and Meanings
page 85
1. Canada
2. Mexico
3. Argentina
4. Brazil
5. Zambia
6. Botswana
7. Germany
8. Switzerland
9. Ireland
10. Belgium
11. Great Britain
12. Israel
13. Pakistan
14. Vietnam
15. Thailand

Word Works
16. Iraqi
17. Norwegian
18. Japanese
19. Turkish
20. Peruvian

Word Play
page 86
1–8. Belgium, Canada, Switzerland, Mexico, Thailand, Germany, Ireland, Brazil
9. Great Britain
10. Zambia
11. Vietnam
12. Botswana
13. Israel
14. Pakistan
15. Argentina

Write on Your Own
page 87
Lists will vary. Students should use four Core Words. Check to see that students have included a reason for visiting every country they cite.

Proofreading Practice
1–4. Mexico, Brazil, Switzerland, Thailand

REVIEW LESSON 24

1. security
2. humidity
3. injury
4. unity
5. kindness
6. loneliness
7. amusement
8. enchantment
9. inflate
10. import
11. immerse
12. inhale
13. fraction
14. numerator
15. multiplication
16. quotient
17. Israel
18. Botswana
19. Belgium
20. Vietnam

LESSON 25

Focus
page 90

1–5. possession, depression, invention, reaction, digestion
6–15. decision, vegetation, occupation, satisfaction, admission, disposition, suspension, absorption, definition, permission
16–20. conce(ss)ion, reco(mm)endation, inte(rr)uption, extension, c(oo)peration

Words and Meanings
page 91

1. permission
2. reaction
3. possession
4. absorption
5. suspension
6. disposition
7. depression
8. decision
9. occupation
10. admission
11. digestion
12. invention
13. satisfaction
14. vegetation
15. definition

Word Works
16. instruction
17. contribution
18. opposition

Word Play
page 92

1–5. decision, reaction, satisfaction, definition, digestion
6. suspension
7. disposition
8. depression
9. invention
10–11. vegetation, occupation
12. absorption
13–14. admission, permission
15. possession

Write on Your Own
page 93

Letters will vary. Students should use four Core Words. Check letters for persuasive reasons to be hired. Emphasize the importance of spelling and proper letter form in an application letter.

Proofreading Practice
1–4. permission, occupation, possession, decision

LESSON 26

Focus
page 94

1–10. abundance, reluctance, defiance, allowance, distance, annoyance, resistance, disturbance, endurance, guidance
11–15. patience, experience, dependence, violence, convenience
16–20. Underlined elements may vary.
compli(ance), appear(ance), intellig(ence), consequ(ence), acquaint(ance)

Words and Meanings
page 95

1. reluctance
2. experience
3. endurance
4. distance
5. convenience
6. abundance
7. annoyance
8. patience
9. dependence
10. disturbance
11. guidance
12. allowance
13. defiance
14. resistance
15. violence

Word Works
16. abundance
17. annoyance
18. reluctance
19. guidance
20. distance

Word Play
page 96

1. patience
2. annoyance
3. resistance
4. dependence
5. abundance
6. reluctance
7. convenience
8. experience
9. distance
10. guidance
11. defiance
12. disturbance
13–14. defiance, violence
15. endurance
16. allowance
17. discount or reduction
18. a sum of money or quantity of something given at regular times or set aside for a particular purpose
19. something that gives ease or comfort
20. ease and comfort

Write on Your Own
page 97

Police reports will vary. Students should use four Core Words. Check to see that students have used precise language.

Proofreading Practice
1–5. disturbance, convenience, distance, resistance, violence

---

LESSON 27

Focus
page 98

1–9. preview, prearrange, prehistoric, predict, premature, preparation, precaution, preface, prefix
10–15. propose, proclamation, progress, provoke, projection, procedure
16–20. (pre)cedent, (pro)cession, (pre)scribe, (pre)occupied, (pre)monition

Words and Meanings
page 99

1. prehistoric
2. predict
3. preparation
4. prearrange
5. propose
6. procedure
7. precaution
8. projection
9. progress
10. provoke
11. premature
12. prefix
13. preview
14. proclamation
15. preface

Word Works
16. like a meteor
17. having to do with athletes
18. having to do with the economy
19. like a nomad
20. having to do with a volcano

Word Play
page 100

1–4. progress, preface, prearrange, procedure
5. premature
6. propose
7. prefix
8. precaution
9. proclamation
10. preview
11. provoke
12. prehistoric
13. projection
14. predict
15. preparation

Write on Your Own
page 101

Journal entries will vary. Students should use four Core Words. Check entries for a logical order of events.
1–4. progress, premature, predict, provoke
5. amazing!
6. Flagstaff, Arizona,

LESSON 28

Focus
page 102

Circled elements may vary.
1–3. w(ei)rd, y(ach)t, c(ough)
4–11. c(ol)onel, s(er)g(ean)t, de(s)ert, de(ss)ert, thor(ough), sh(e)ri(ff), (sc)i(ss)ors, sol(di)er
12–15. te(rr)i(f)ic, o(cc)asion, emba(rr)a(ss), o(cc)u(rr)ence
16–20. aqu(ar)ium, mo(cc)asin, g(au)ge, accident(all)y, bro(cco)li

Words and Meanings
page 103

1. sheriff
2. colonel/sergeant
3. sergeant/colonel
4. soldier
5. desert
6. terrific
7. occasion
8. occurrence
9. cough
10. yacht
11. embarrass
12. weird
13. thorough
14. scissors
15. dessert

Word Works
16. stationery/stationary
17. colonel/kernel
18. alter/altar
19. desert/dessert
20. coarse/course

Word Play
page 104

1–2. occasion, occurrence
3. sheriff
4–6. terrific, embarrass, occurrence
7–9. dessert, embarrass, scissors
10. thorough
11. yacht
12. weird
13. cough
14. colonel
15. soldier
16. sergeant
17. scissors
18. desert
19. a hot, dry, sandy area of land with few or no plants growing on it
20. to go away and leave a person or thing that should not be left
21. to feed on growing grass
22. to scrape or touch lightly in passing

Write on Your Own
page 105

Story endings will vary. Students should use four Core Words. Check for interesting story endings.

Proofreading Practice
1–4. sergeant, colonel, desert, embarrass

LESSON 29

Focus
page 106
1–15. *bi-*: biceps, binoculars, biannual; *mono-*: monotone, monopoly, monorail; *tri-*: triplets, triangle, tricycle, triplicate; *uni-*: universe, uniform, unicorn, unison, unicycle
16–20. (tri)angular, (bi)centennial, (uni)que, (tri)pod, (mono)polize

Words and Meanings
page 107
1. biannual
2. monopoly
3. universe
4. uniform
5. unicycle
6. monorail
7. triplets
8. triplicate
9. tricycle
10. triangle
11. biceps
12. monotone
13. unicorn
14. binoculars
15. unison

Word Works
16. tricolor
17. monoplane
18. bimonthly

Word Play
page 108
1–8. monorail, monotone, tricycle, uniform, unicorn, triangle, unicycle, monopoly
9. triplicate
10. triplets
11. binoculars
12. biceps
13. unison
14. universe
15. biannual

Write on Your Own
page 109
Sales pitches will vary. Students should use four Core Words. This assignment provides an opportunity for students to use new and interesting adjectives. Check for these when reviewing their papers.

Proofreading Practice
1–5. triplets, unison, tricycle, universe, monopoly

REVIEW LESSON 30

1. occupation
2. possession
3. depression
4. definition
5. patience
6. convenience
7. reluctance
8. distance
9. prefix
10. provoke
11. prehistoric
12. progress
13. colonel
14. yacht
15. weird
16. dessert
17. tricycle
18. binoculars
19. uniform
20. monotone

LESSON 31

Focus
page 112
1–6. active, protective, destructive, detective, expressive, defective
7–15. exclusive, creative, informative, captive, aggressive, comparative, defensive, alternative, conclusive
16–20. cooperat(ive), abras(ive), cumulat(ive), descript(ive), communicat(ive)

Words and Meanings
page 113
1. informative
2. conclusive
3. exclusive
4. creative
5. defensive
6. alternative
7. captive
8. protective
9. destructive
10. detective
11. defective
12. expressive/active
13. comparative
14. aggressive
15. active

Word Works
16. aggressive
17. captive
18. defective
19. destructive
20. defensive

Word Play
page 114
1–7. detective, active, exclusive, defective, creative, expressive, comparative
8. protective
9. informative
10. defensive
11. alternative
12. aggressive
13. destructive
14. conclusive
15. captive

Write on Your Own
page 115
Letters will vary. Students should use four Core Words. Check to see if students have used the correct business letter format.

Proofreading Practice
1–4. exclusive, aggressive, defective, alternative

LESSON 32

Focus
page 116
NOTE: Circled elements may vary.
1–8. sub(urban), sub(due), subsequent, sub(marine), substitute, sub(merge), substance, subscribe
9–15. super(highway), superior, superstition, supervise, superb, super(market), supersonic
16–20. (super)sede, (sub)conscious, (super)lative, (sub)terranean, (super)intendent

Words and Meanings
page 117
1. supermarket
2. substance
3. superhighway
4. substitute
5. superior
6. suburban
7. superstition
8. supersonic
9. subdue
10. submarine
11. supervise
12. submerge
13. superb
14. subsequent
15. subscribe

Word Works
16. subway
17. subnormal
18. subsoil
19. subtopic
20. subheading

Word Play
page 118
1. supervise
2. superior
3. supersonic
4. superhighway
5. submarine
6. subdue
7. subsequent
8. submerge
9. subscribe
10. supermarket
11–12. suburban, superb
13–15. superstition, substitute, substance
16. su/p(e)r/sti/ti(o)n
17. sub/m(a)r/ine
18. s(u)b/scribe
19. s(u)b/ur/b(a)n
20. s(u)/pe/ri/(o)r

Write on Your Own
page 119
Tall tales will vary. Students should use four Core Words. Check that each story has a beginning, middle, and end.

Proofreading Practice
1–5. superhighway, supersonic, substance, suburban, subscribe

LESSON 33

Focus
page 120
1–7. co(mm)ission, co(mm)unicate, co(mm)i(tt)ee, company, complicate, co(mm)unity, compound
8–11. co(ll)apse, co(ll)ide, co(ll)ege, co(ll)ection
12–15. conservation, concentrate, co(nn)ect, conclusion
16–20. (com)promise, (con)ference, (con)vey, (com)mencement, (con)spiracy

Words and Meanings
page 121
1. collide
2. collapse
3. community
4. concentrate
5. collection
6. conservation
7. commission/committee
8. committee/commission
9. communicate
10. college
11. company
12. compound
13. connect
14. complicate
15. conclusion

Word Works
16. confront
17. composition
18. colleague
19. commend
20. conjunction
21. combine
22. constellation

Word Play
page 122
1. conservation
2. college
3. conclusion
4. commission
5. committee
6. collide
7–9. communicate, concentrate, complicate
10–11. company, community
12. compound
13–14. connect, collection
15. collapse

Write on Your Own
page 123
Lists will vary. Students should use four Core Words. Check to see that students have used strong, clear verbs.

Proofreading Practice
1–4. community, concentrate, collection, commission

LESSON 34

Focus
page 124
Underlined elements may vary.
1–4. supreme, brill(iant), awesome, dazzl(ing)
5–11. wonderful, marvelous, astounding, fantas(tic), cham(pion), ideal, out(standing)
12–15. valu(able), remarkable, incredible, admir(able)
16–20. miraculous, (extraordinary), magnificent, spectacular, (praiseworthy)

Words and Meanings
page 125
1. fantastic
2. dazzling
3. remarkable
4. wonderful
5. brilliant
6. admirable
7. valuable
8. incredible
9. astounding
10. marvelous
11. ideal
12. outstanding
13. champion
14. awesome
15. supreme

Word Works
16. outfield
17. outsmart
18. outlaw
19. outcome
20. outgoing

Word Play
page 126
1. marvelous
2. outstanding
3. fantastic
4. wonderful
5. remarkable
6. brilliant/dazzling
7. astounding
8. ideal
9. incredible
10. supreme
11. greatness
12. awesome
13–17. fantastic, champion, valuable, dazzling, admirable
18. dazzle
19. crazy
20. comedy

Write on Your Own
page 127
Reviews will vary. Students should use four Core Words. The assignment provides an opportunity to see if students are formulating good topic sentences.

Proofreading Practice
1–5. awesome, champion, brilliant, fantastic, dazzling

LESSON 35

Focus
page 128
Circled and underlined elements may vary.
1–4. lei(sure), baggage, journey, tour(ist)
5–10. ar(range)(ment)s, vaca(tion), museum, (rest)aurant, excur(sion), (pass)eng(er)
11–15. trans(port)a(tion), recrea(tion), reserva(tion), cancella(tion), unusual
16–20. (tr)avelogue, atte(nd)a(nt), e(sc)ape, (br)ochure, vagabo(nd)

Words and Meanings
page 129
1. vacation
2. leisure
3. journey
4. unusual
5. tourist
6. museum
7. arrangements
8. cancellation
9. reservation
10. restaurant
11. excursion
12. transportation
13. passenger
14. recreation
15. baggage

Word Works
16. violinist
17. novelist
18. colonist
19. cyclist
20. motorist

Word Play
page 130
1. restaurant
2. museum
3. unusual
4. transportation
5. arrangements
6. tourist
7. passenger
8. leisure
9. baggage
10. excursion
11. reservation
12. cancellation
13. journey
14. vacation
15. recreation
16. lei-sure
17. res-tau-rant
18. jour-ney
19. trans-por-ta-tion
20. ex-cur-sion

Write on Your Own
page 131
Postcards will vary. Students should use four Core Words. Check students' work for correct capitalization and punctuation.

Proofreading Practice
1–4. vacation, excursion, passenger, journey
5. London, England
6. was?

REVIEW LESSON 36

1. alternative
2. creative
3. captive
4. destructive
5. supermarket
6. submarine
7. subsequent
8. supervise
9. connect
10. complicate
11. collide
12. conclusion
13. brilliant
14. fantastic
15. valuable
16. marvelous
17. tourist
18. journey
19. restaurant
20. leisure